The life of Debussy

Musical lives

The books in this series will each provide
an account of the life of a major composer,
considering both the private and the public
figure. The main thread will be biographical,
and discussion of the music will be integral
to the narrative. Each book thus presents an
organic view of the composer, the music,
and the circumstances in which it was written.

Published titles

The life of Debussy

ROGER NICHOLS

CAMBRIDGE
UNIVERSITY PRESS

PUBLISHED BY THE PRESS SYNDICATE OF THE UNIVERSITY OF CAMBRIDGE
The Pitt Building, Trumpington Street, Cambridge CB2 1RP, United Kingdom

CAMBRIDGE UNIVERSITY PRESS
The Edinburgh Building, Cambridge, CB2 2RU, United Kingdom
40 West 20th Street, New York, NY 10011-4211, USA
10 Stamford Road, Oakleigh, Melbourne 3166, Australia

First published 1998

Printed in the United Kingdom at the University Press, Cambridge

Typeset in FF Quadraat 9.75/14 pt, in QuarkXPress™ [SE]

A catalogue record for this book is available from the British Library

Library of Congress cataloguing in publication data

Nichols, Roger.
     Life of Debussy / Roger Nichols.
          p.   cm. – (Musical lives; 4)
     Includes index.
     ISBN 0 521 57026 3 hardback – ISBN 0 521 57887 6 paperback
          1. Debussy, Claude, 1862–1918.   2. Composers – France – Biography.
     I. Title.   II. Series.
     ML410.D28N55   1998
     780'.92 – DC21

CONTENTS

ILLUSTRATIONS

ACKNOWLEDGEMENTS

I am glad to express my indebtedness to the other members of the five Rs, Robin Holloway, Roy Howat, Richard Langham Smith and Robert Orledge, whose combined expertise and enthusiasm have contributed so much to our knowledge of Debussy and his music and who have, wittingly or not, through their writings and through many friendly conversations, started several of the hares pursued in this book. They cannot be held responsible for the success or otherwise of these pursuits.

Author's note
To avoid burdening the pages with reference numbers, I have made efforts to include in the text itself enough information to enable those readers who want to follow up references to do so. Debussy's newspaper articles can be found in English translation in *Debussy on Music*; his letters likewise in *Debussy Letters*; and reminiscences from friends and contemporaries in *Debussy Remembered*. Details of these and other relevant volumes in English may be found in Further Reading at the back of the book, pp. 174–6 below.

Prologue

To the reader

Do you play 'The Girl with the Flaxen Hair'? Or the 'Golliwogg's Cake Walk'? If so, and that is all, then you could well think of Debussy as a minor talent, a gifted miniaturist. But even within these narrow confines more is going on than you might at first suppose. The central section of the 'Golliwogg' is a (more or less?) affectionate skit on Wagner's *Tristan and Isolde*; while Leconte de Lisle's poem 'La fille aux cheveux de lin', which inspired Debussy's seemingly cool prelude, is itself very far from cool – 'I want', says the poet, 'to kiss the blond of your hair and press the purple of your lips.' For more than a century now, performers, writers and analysts have been peeling away the layers of the onion that is Debussy. I think it is some measure of his greatness that the more we peel, the more we find. Certainly, if you ever thought being a composer was an easy road, a harmless hobby, an irrelevance, an opt out from the serious things of life, I would ask you to read on . . .

1 Childhood and musical studies (1862–1884)

Another man's soul is a thick forest in which one must walk with
circumspection

(Claude Debussy)

To understand something of the France into which Achille-Claude
Debussy was born on 22 August 1862, we need to go back a few years –
say, to 2 December 1851, when Louis-Napoleon dissolved the French
Assembly and seized power in a *coup d'état*. Thirty years after Napoleon
Bonaparte's death, the family name still had the power to move and
what became known as the Second Empire began with high hopes in
many quarters, political, social and artistic.

The forty-eight-year-old Hector Berlioz greeted the *coup d'état* as a
'masterstroke', and a month later could enthuse to his sister that
Louis-Napoleon was 'going from strength to strength, he is realizing
all my dreams about the government. He is sublime in his reasoning,
his logic, his steadfastness and his decisiveness.' At the same time he
felt obliged to sound one slightly cautionary note: 'I'm certain that for
all official ceremonies . . . he will always choose men of the Establishment, old men and old works.'[1]

As it turned out, Berlioz's caution was better justified than his
enthusiasm. Almost exactly four years later, and with exception made
for only four composers including Saint-Saëns and Gounod, he confessed that on the musical front he saw 'nothing but flies hovering

above this stinking bog called Paris'.[2] A look at the operatic premieres in Paris that year (1856) lend this jaundiced view some support: Bottesini's *L'assedio di Firenze*, Auber's *Manon Lescaut*, Clapisson's *La fanchonnette*, Adam's *Les pantins de Violette*, Maillart's *Les dragons de Villars*, Bazin's *Maître Pathelin*, Massé's *La reine Topaze* – where are they now?

Things improved somewhat towards the end of the decade, as Gounod lived up to Berlioz's hopes for him with *Le médecin malgré lui* in 1858 and *Faust* the following year. But the temper of the times can be more accurately read in the other hit of the decade, Offenbach's *Orphée aux enfers* (Orpheus in the Underworld), which in 1858 ran at the Bouffes-Parisiens theatre for 227 consecutive nights. In this and subsequent works, Offenbach achieved a blend of catchy tunes and social satire that would not be matched until the Brecht/Weill collaborations of sixty years later. In that insidious way that music has, Offenbach's operettas began to render criticism of Louis-Napoleon's regime increasingly respectable, so that when Bismarck visited the 1867 Paris Universal Exhibition and was encouraged by the manifest evidence of France's corruption and complacency to consider his own 'cleaning-up' operation, his views, if not his solutions, were shared by many Frenchmen.

All in all, the decade into which Debussy was born must rate as one of the low points of French musical life. In 1861, *Tannhäuser* had been whistled off the stage of the Opéra after only three performances and a year later Berlioz, writing indeed the day before Debussy's birth, reflected on the success of his opera *Béatrice et Bénédict* – in Baden-Baden; adding 'the cliques and detractors stayed in Paris'.[3]

We owe most of the details of Debussy's forebears to the meticulous research carried out by the Swiss scholar Marcel Dietschy for his biography published in 1962, the composer's centenary year.[4] Until the late 1790s the de Bussy family (as they then spelt the name) were Burgundian peasants. It was the composer's great-grandfather Pierre, born in 1768, who made the move to Paris. His fourth child,

Claude-Alexandre, the composer's grandfather and a carpenter, was born in 1812 and had nine children, the two eldest of whom, as Dietschy records, 'played a role in Debussy's life: Manuel-Achille, his father, and Clémentine, godmother, benefactress, and prophesier of his future'. After a move out of Paris in 1823, Claude-Alexandre moved back to the capital in 1848 and his daughter Clémentine opened a 'Maison Debussy, couture'. The more democratic spelling of the surname appears to date from this time (perhaps Paris was a hard place in which to maintain affectations of aristocracy), although a distant cousin of the composer, living in Leeds in 1960, was still calling himself de Bussy.

Debussy's father, Manuel-Achille, was twelve at the time of the family's return to Paris in 1848. One may, of course, speculate about the effects on a boy of that age of the year's revolutionary activities. Be that as it may, Manuel-Achille was to lead what may politely be termed an irregular existence, and for the first ten years of the composer's life made a living in turn as a seller of china, a broker, a clerk in a printing works and a civil servant.

Debussy's mother, born Victorine Manoury and also of Burgundian stock, had been Manuel-Achille's mistress before marrying him on 30 November 1861. They immediately moved to the western outskirts of Paris, to Saint-Germain-en-Laye, where Achille-Claude was born nine months later. In view of doubts expressed by later writers over the composer's paternity, it may be as well to say that a comparison of a portrait of Debussy on his deathbed with one of his grandfather Claude-Alexandre lays all such doubts to rest.

For some reason, Achille-Claude was not baptised until 31 July 1864, just before his second birthday. His godparents were his aunt Clémentine and her then 'protector' Achille-Antoine Arosa, a thirty-five-year-old Paris stockjobber. He seems to have taken some interest in his godson in his earliest years, at least until around 1866 or possibly 1868 when his liaison with Clémentine ended. After that Arosa seems to have developed an antipathy to his godson. His son Paul told Dietschy in 1954 that Arosa could not stand the young Debussy's 'distant manner' (*l'air distant*) and behind his back referred to him as *l'Arsouille*, defined in Larousse as *voyou et debauché* (yob and debauchee).

According to a family friend, Debussy's mother was a very independent woman who 'found her children an irritating burden and kept out of their way as far as she could' and who farmed out at least two of them to her sister-in-law. But Achille-Claude was one of the ones she kept with her and there was no doubt that he enjoyed the dubious advantage of being her favourite: for one thing, he was alone of his siblings in not going to school and his first taste of formal tuition was to come at the Paris Conservatoire, when he was already ten years old. According to Debussy's step-daughter Mme de Tinan, who knew both his parents, he learnt to read and write from his mother, who 'was very severe with her children, frequently slapping them, an unpleasant memory that her sons recalled laughingly'.[5]

What music the young Achille-Claude may have heard in the 1860s remains a matter of conjecture. His father was quite fond of operetta but forty years later, in 1907, Debussy confided to his friend Victor Segalen in October 1907 that 'my father intended me for the sea. Then he met somebody . . . I don't know how it happened. "Ah! He can play that? Very good. But he must be taught music . . ." etc. So my father then got the idea that I should study just music, he being someone who knew nothing about it.'

Debussy's first documented musical experience dates from his visits to his aunt Clémentine in Cannes in 1870 and 1871. He later told his first biographer, Louis Laloy,[6] that in the latter year he began piano lessons with a violinist called Jean Cerutti. More precisely, he indicated to Laloy that his aunt 'eut la fantaisie' (had the strange idea) of getting him to learn the piano. Although typical of the mature Debussy's ironic way of expressing himself, this does seem to suggest that until that point he had given no particular indication of musical interests. Indeed, his sister Adèle, who was in Cannes with him, remembered that he would spend some time playing with her cardboard theatre (premonitions of the boy Messiaen forty years later!),

1   Debussy aged five years. © P. Willy, Paris

but that more often he would spend 'entire days sitting in a chair dreaming, no one knew what about'. We may speculate that this early absorption of the piano into days of reverie was to leave its mark throughout his life.

Meanwhile, in Paris and northern France, events unfolded leading to the Franco-Prussian War and, in March 1871, to the Commune. Debussy referred, in a letter to his publisher Jacques Durand of 8 August 1914, to his 'memory of '70, which prevents me from yielding to enthusiasm', but it seems likely that it was the events of '71 which left a deeper scar – and that, not for the only time, Debussy was quietly re-arranging facts to suit himself. The real truth was that his father joined the Communards, became a captain and led an attack on the fort at Issy. He was arrested, released and then, when the Commune was defeated on 22 May, imprisoned. In December he was tried and sentenced to four years in jail. He served one year of the sentence, which was then commuted to four years' deprivation of civic, civil and familial rights. It would seem therefore that the family's visit to Cannes in 1871 (Laloy, relaying information from Debussy, says that he was there 'with his parents') must have taken place shortly after Manuel-Achille had completed his year in prison at Satory. Again, one may hazard that Achille-Claude might easily have fixated on the piano and on music as constants in a disturbingly mobile world.

While in the Satory prison, Manuel-Achille met a fellow prisoner Charles de Sivry, described in a police report (perhaps not unbiassed) as a 'distinguished musician, member of all the secret societies . . . bad poet . . . a very harmful person'. Harmful or not, he had a sister, Mathilde, who had married Paul Verlaine in 1870 and a mother, calling herself Mme Mauté de Fleurville, who claimed to have been a piano pupil of Chopin. (It could be said of every small French town in the latter part of the nineteenth century that it contained at least one *soi-disant* Chopin pupil, just as every small American town in the 1950s contained, if we are to believe Aaron Copland, a 10-cent store and a pupil of Nadia Boulanger.)

It has long been established that Mme Mauté does not figure on any official list of Chopin's pupils. But, perhaps more to the point, all Debussy's future references to her were to be marked by appreciation and gratitude. He explained to Alfredo Casella 'how considerable a part this instruction had played in his musical formation, not only as pianist, but also as creator' and to his publisher Jacques Durand that she recommended 'practising without pedal and, in performance, not holding it on except in very rare instances. It was the same way of turning the pedal into a kind of *breathing* which I observed in Liszt when I had the chance to hear him in Rome.'[7] Whether or not this recommendation came initially from Chopin, as Mme Mauté had claimed, a comparison with Liszt is no mean testimonial. Nor is the fact that the playing of the ten-year-old Debussy was good enough to get him accepted by the Paris Conservatoire at the first attempt on 22 October 1872.

The Conservatoire had been founded on 16 thermidor Year III (3 August 1795), incorporating the Institut national de musique founded two years earlier and the Ecole nationale de chant et de déclamation. The patriotic aim was to set up an institution to rival the best Italian conservatories. The *Journal de Paris* of 27 October 1796 expressed the hope that 'the tyranny of routine would be banished, as well as the licentiousness of innovations. The respect due to the works of deserving masters will be maintained, without refusing a warm welcome to the daring of genius and to the fruits of happy inspiration (*aux heureuses créations*).'

This balance looks very fine on paper (and, over two centuries later, is still accepted by Conservatoire Directors as an ideal to aim at), but in the course of the nineteenth century the Conservatoire came to stand more for conservation than for experiment, and as a centre for training composers rather of opera than of symphonies or chamber music – this last an unsurprising penchant since its three Directors until 1896 (Cherubini, Auber and Ambroise Thomas) had all made their names in the opera house. But whatever its faults, under Cherubini's firm guidance the Conservatoire soon become the place for an aspiring French composer to attend. Of the attempts to rival it, or to supplement its opera-based training, only two in the nineteenth century had any success: the Ecole Niedermeyer, set up in 1853 to train organists and choirmasters, and the Schola Cantorum, founded in 1894 by Vincent d'Indy and others to study the music of the past and in general to give a more rounded training than the Conservatoire could provide.

When Debussy entered the institution in 1872, Ambroise Thomas had been in post for only a year. If he is remembered at all nowadays, apart from his opera *Mignon*, it is because he refused to appoint Fauré as a composition professor, or for the quips of Satie and Chabrier ('there are three sorts of music: good music, bad music and the music of Ambroise Thomas'). But even if his directorship of the Conservatoire, ended by his death in 1896, was not marked by any revolutionary experiments, he was at least highly conscientious and in 1894 he became the first musician to be elevated to the Grand Croix of the Légion d'honneur.

On Friday, 25 October 1872 Debussy attended his first Conservatoire piano class. His teacher was the fifty-six-year-old Antoine François Marmontel (not to be confused with his son, Antoine Emile, who taught the piano at the Conservatoire from 1901). Marmontel *père* had been a piano professor there since 1848 and was highly regarded as a teacher: apart from Debussy, his pupils included Bizet, Albéniz, d'Indy and the virtuoso Francis Planté. He seems to have been an exacting master and relations with Debussy were sometimes strained, especially when Marmontel insisted on fitting the words 'O mère, douleur amère!' to the Rondo theme in Beethoven's *Pathétique* Sonata. Beethoven was never to be Debussy's favourite composer, and we may surmise that he found his mother quite difficult enough at home without being reminded of her in class as well.

One of the sharpest and most engaging portraits of Debussy in his early years at the Conservatoire comes from Gabriel Pierné, his junior by almost exactly a year and destined for a solid career in Paris as composer and conductor: he was to conduct the first performance of

Debussy's *Ibéria* in 1910 and the first concert performance of *Jeux* in 1914:

> I got to know Debussy around 1873 in Lavignac's *solfège* class at the Conservatoire. He was a fat boy of ten or so, short, thickset, wearing a black coat enlivened by a loose, spotted tie and short, velvet trousers . . . His clumsiness and awkwardness were extraordinary, in addition to which he was shy and even unsociable.
>
> In Marmontel's piano class he used to astound us with his bizarre playing. Whether it was through natural maladroitness or through shyness I don't know, but he literally used to charge at the piano and force all his effects. He seemed to be in a rage with the instrument, rushing up and down it with impulsive gestures and breathing noisily during the difficult bits. These faults gradually receded and occasionally he would achieve effects of an astonishing softness. With all its faults and virtues, his playing remained something highly individual.

The *solfège* teacher Pierné refers to was Albert Lavignac. He had been a pupil of Ambroise Thomas at the Conservatoire and, when Thomas was appointed Director in 1871, he immediately asked his twenty-five-year-old ex-pupil to plan a new course in sight-reading and musical dictation. Lavignac's exercises were not for the faint-hearted, involving as they did use of all seven traditional clefs and transposition at sight and at speed.

Lavignac was already a Wagner lover (in 1897 he was to publish his *Voyage artistique à Bayreuth*) and was happy to pass on his enthusiasm to his pupils. One winter's evening, Debussy and his teacher became so absorbed in reading the *Tannhäuser* Overture that they were locked in and had to find their way out of the Conservatoire in the dark. A brief extract from the first chapter of Lavignac's book *L'éducation musicale* of 1902 suggests that his teaching enshrined the same blend of ortho-doxy and liberalism found in the Conservatoire's original aims. 'Like all languages', he wrote, 'music possesses various dialects, patois or jargons, it even has its slang. As to the ways of writing it down, these can be rational and etymological, phonetic, or whimsical (*fantaisistes*).

One can therefore speak it more, or less, well and write it more, or less, correctly ... Finally, like all languages, it transforms itself continually through slow, logical evolution, following the progress of civilisation and corresponding to the needs of different times and places.'[8]

All in all, Debussy's early years at the Conservatoire were remarkably successful, given his individualism and propensity for blunt speaking – 'one is suffocated by your rhythms', he once complained to Lavignac. With hindsight we can say that the student was lucky in these two teachers. In 1874 he won a third medal for *solfège* and a second certificate of merit in the piano exam, playing Chopin's F minor Piano Concerto; in 1875 he won a second medal for *solfège* and a first certificate playing Chopin's Second Ballade; in 1876 he finally gained the first medal in *solfège*. That year his piano playing failed to impress, but he did win the second prize in the summer of 1877.

By now it had become clear to Debussy's father that his eldest son might, for all his dreamy ways, have a future as a concert pianist. From what the composer said later, these 'castles in the air' occupied a good deal of his father's waking thoughts and a certain amount of unwelcome and probably counterproductive pressure was brought to bear on Achille-Claude to practise more. But Marmontel had got the measure of his pupil. 'He doesn't care much for the piano', he wrote, 'but he does love music.' No prizes came Debussy's way in 1878 or 1879, failures which disqualified him from trying again, and those particular paternal visions vanished for ever.

But outside the Conservatoire Debussy's musical horizons began to expand, thanks to Marmontel's support. In the summer of 1879 he got Debussy a job playing in the castle of Chenonceaux for a rich lady who was the mistress of the President, Jules Grévy. Then, in 1880, he found Debussy a place in the entourage of Nadezhda von Meck, Tchaikovsky's patroness. On 10 July 1880, she wrote to Tchaikovsky from Interlaken:

> The day before yesterday there arrived from Paris a young pianist who has just won a first prize in Marmontel's class at the Conservatoire. I've engaged him for the summer, to give lessons to the children, to

accompany [her daughter] Julia's singing and to play piano duets with me. The young man plays well, his technique is brilliant, but he's lacking in sensibility. He's still too young. He says he's twenty, but looks sixteen.

Clearly Debussy was determined to hold his own in the high-powered atmosphere of the von Meck household and was not above indulging in a little *fantaisie* of his own – as we know, he never won a first prize for piano and at the time he was not twenty but rising eighteen. But Madame von Meck liked him and he further won her over by his praise of Tchaikovsky's music, saying of the fugue in Tchaikovsky's First Orchestral Suite 'M. Massenet wouldn't be able to do anything like it' (which might even have been true). He also, in a letter of 7 August 1880, took up his definitive position with regard to the Germans, who 'don't have our temperament, they're so heavy and unclear'. The use of the word 'our' to denote a Franco-Russian musical axis was probably not just a case of Debussy being diplomatic. Russian music, in its many manifestations, was to impinge frequently in the coming years both on his own music and on that of his younger rival Maurice Ravel.

Debussy returned to the von Mecks during the summer and early autumn of 1881 and 1882. These journeys took him not just to Moscow and elsewhere in Russia but to Interlaken, Rome, Naples and Vienna. On 28 August 1882, a few days after Debussy really did reach his twentieth birthday, Mme von Meck wrote to Tchaikovsky:

> Yesterday, to my great joy, Achille Debussy arrived. Now I shall gorge myself listening to music, and he'll bring the whole house to life. He's a Parisian to his fingertips, a real *gamin de Paris*, as witty as they come and a brilliant mimic. He takes Gounod and Ambroise Thomas off perfectly, he makes you die laughing.

But if Debussy's sense of humour remained the same as ever, his outlook on the future had changed. Whether or not he had ever shared his father's hopes for him as a piano virtuoso, those were now dashed beyond retrieval. Already, he had made up his mind to be a composer.

The Conservatoire's rules insisted that pupils needed at least one first prize in the area of music theory before they were allowed to proceed to the composition classes proper. Once again, though, we have to guess as to whether intention on Debussy's part brought about a fact or vice versa. In the autumn of 1879 he had entered the class given by Auguste-Ernest Bazille in practical keyboard harmony and score-reading and in the examination the following summer he gained the first prize that he needed.

On Christmas Eve 1880, not long back from his first stay with Madame von Meck, he enrolled as a composition student in the class of Ernest Guiraud. Guiraud's father, a composer, had left Paris in the 1830s for New Orleans, despairing of ever seeing any work of his on a Paris stage. Ernest was brought up in New Orleans, but came to Paris in his teens and was another Marmontel pupil at the Conservatoire. When Debussy joined his class, he had been in post only a couple of months, replacing Victor Massé who had just resigned through ill health.

Nowadays Guiraud enjoys the perhaps dubious distinction of having turned the spoken dialogue in *Carmen* into recitative. But he succeeded where his father had failed, with three of his *opéras-comiques* reaching the Paris stage between 1873 and 1882. His friend Bizet described him as 'so nice, so friendly, but a little soft, a little apathetic' and he seems never to have locked horns with Debussy, but to have smiled quizzically at his more outrageous ideas, ventured a few comments and left it at that. The two men remained friends until Guiraud's early death in 1892. The notes taken by another pupil, Maurice Emmanuel, of conversations between Debussy and Guiraud around 1890 will be discussed in Chapter 3.

Unlike many composers, Debussy seems not to have spent his early teens covering sheet after sheet of manuscript paper with symphonies, concertos and aborted five-act operas. No work of his can be definitely dated before the song 'Madrid' dating from the spring of 1879, when he was sixteen and a half, while his first extended work, the Piano Trio in G, was written during September and October 1880.

No doubt his entry into a composition class in December 1880 concentrated his mind to some extent on the desirability of settling down to composition in regular and disciplined fashion, and during the three and a half years he remained in Guiraud's class he did produce a number of compositions of an academic cast. But an earlier and stronger impulse, from outside the Conservatoire's walls, guided him from the autumn of 1880.

He got back to Paris in the middle of October and, to help with his precarious finances, took on a job as an accompanist for singing classes held by Madame Moreau-Sainti. She had made her debut at the Opéra in 1856 in a revival of Verdi's *Les Vêpres siciliennes* and was now a fifty-three-year-old widow. Debussy wrote his song 'Nuit d'étoiles', on a poem by Théodore de Banville, in the September and October of 1880 – that is to say, he at least began it while staying with Madame von Meck. But he dedicated it to Madame Moreau-Sainti.

Among her pupils was Marie-Blanche Vasnier: no fifty-three-year-old widow, but a thirty-two-year-old woman married at seventeen to a legal expert eleven years her senior; and with the green eyes Debussy was always to find irresistible. There were no more dedications to Madame Moreau-Sainti . . .

The dating of Debussy's early songs is still slightly unsure, but the first songs we know he wrote for and dedicated to Marie-Blanche Vasnier come from 1881. It may be tempting to include in them another song from the end of 1880 on a Banville poem, even though her name is not officially attached to it: 'Aimons-nous et dormons', whose title goes on to specify in somewhat Verlainian fashion 'sans songer au reste du monde' (without thinking about the rest of the world). But her tally is long enough without conjectural additions: between the early months of 1881 and February 1884 Debussy dedicated to her no fewer than twenty-three songs, as well as some extracts, at least, from a setting of a *comédie lyrique*, *Hymnis*, again by Banville.

We learn from contemporary reviews that Madame Vasnier had a light voice, with considerable agility in the upper register, and that she sang to a fully professional standard. Debussy, we may be sure, would not otherwise have written for her, however green her eyes. The songs composed in 1881 and the first half of 1882, such as 'Jane', 'Sérénade' or the sprightly 'Pierrot', show Debussy working in the Gounod/ Massenet idiom, taking no risks and exuding a fairly all-purpose charm. To some extent this stems too from the poetry itself, 'Jane' being a setting of Leconte de Lisle and the other two, yet again, of Banville and from the volume *Les cariatides* published by the eighteen-year-old poet in 1842.

Since Debussy never went to school before joining the Conservatoire in 1872, and since his mother, apart from teaching him to read and write, seems to have had no literary bent, we must assume that his early tastes in literature were the result either of contact with his peers and teachers at the Conservatoire or of some kind of instinct which, in bookshops, guided his hand to one volume rather than another. Whatever the truth, he clearly found in the poetry of Banville a kindred voice.

His friend Raymond Bonheur later remembered their first meeting at the Conservatoire: 'we quite soon became friends through a volume of Banville which I found in his hands, a rather surprising discovery in that milieu' – which suggests that Debussy had lighted on Banville through his own initiative. The poet and the composer did indeed have much in common: a fascination with Ancient Greek legend, a high regard for Wagner, a belief that art needed to retain contact with popular sources (as in the song 'Pierrot' mentioned above, in which Debussy quotes the tune 'Au clair de la lune') and a love of the mysterious, the half-expressed. As early as 1846, in his preface to the collection *Les stalactites* (from which Debussy chose the poem for 'Nuit d'étoiles') Banville wrote: 'it would be no more sensible to exclude the half-light (*le demi-jour*) from poetry than it would be reasonable to wish it absent from Nature; and it is necessary, in order to leave certain poetical objects in the gloom (*le crépuscule*) which envelops them and in the atmosphere which impregnates them, to have recourse to the artifices of negligence'.

We may think that, at twenty-three, Banville was a little young to be cultivating 'the artifices of negligence'; at the same time, we can imagine the joy with which any twenty-year-old composer might seize on the idea, and at the same time the problems he might have with a teacher like Lavignac who, as we know, felt one could write music either accurately or inaccurately, with nothing in between.

Even the lenient Guiraud complained in his report on Debussy in January 1883 that 'il écrit mal la musique', a remark that has been given various interpretations. What it certainly could not mean was that Debussy's manuscript was shoddy: even as early as 1880 it was the small, clear, elegant and utterly distinctive hand it would remain. Edward Lockspeiser interprets the phrase to mean that he was said 'to write music clumsily'. That is possible, in the sense that his music may not always have obeyed the rules Guiraud would have liked to impose. But my own feeling is it may simply have meant that he was casual with his accidentals – a fault that persisted, to the irritation of editors ever since. If Debussy did ever succumb to 'the artifices of negligence', they showed not so much in the *facture* of his music as in its effects. An appearance of negligence was, after all, one of the aims of the Baudelairean dandy. And it demanded a very great deal of hard, unseen preparatory work.

As the Conservatoire had been established to some extent under the eye of Napoleon Bonaparte, it was only to be expected that, in the way of that supreme bureaucrat, its budding composers should be given a goal to aim at (what these days would, no doubt, be called a 'course mission statement'). In 1803, the Grand Prix de Rome was instituted. After a preliminary competition in which you had to set a short text for chorus and orchestra and write a fugue on a given subject, the half-dozen or so best candidates went on to the *concours* proper. This consisted of a longer text, the so-called cantata (itself, incidentally, the winner of a competition, unlikely as that might seem from the results), to be set for three soloists and orchestra. For this task candidates were immured for a month (the Château de Compiègne was a favourite venue) in a cell with just a piano and a table. Families were allowed to visit in the courtyard at stated times, under supervision.

The results were first inspected by the six eminent musicians who formed the musical section of the forty members of the Académie des Beaux Arts in the Institut. They passed on a recommendation to the rest of the Institut, before they all attended a performance, with piano accompaniment, of the competing cantatas, to which the general public was also admitted. The winner was given a bursary to study at the Villa Medici in Rome for a minimum of two years, with options for extension and European travel. Unsuccessful candidates could continue to compete, as Ravel did, until they were thirty.

The competition was designed to encourage composers with a flair for the theatre, composers who would then go on to become the glories of the Opéra and the Opéra-Comique. Opinions over the value of the enterprise continued to be divided, sometimes violently, until the Prix de Rome was finally discontinued following the *évènements* of 1968. Until then, proponents could quote winners such as Berlioz, Gounod, Bizet, Massenet, André Caplet, Lili Boulanger and Dutilleux; opponents could point to unsuccessful candidates such as Saint-Saëns, Dukas, Ravel and Messiaen, as well as a hundred and more successful ones whose names had sunk into oblivion.

In the course of the twentieth century, the Conservatoire composition classes developed along two parallel lines. The composition professor André Gedalge, who taught Ravel, Milhaud and Honegger among many others, used to ask students before taking them on whether they wanted to win the Prix de Rome or whether they wanted to learn to compose; if the former, then he would send them to his colleague Caussade. In the 1880s this division did not yet apply, and Guiraud and Massenet were both content to prepare their pupils for the final hurdle, which they themselves had surmounted in 1859 and 1863 respectively.

For any lover of Banville's world of melancholy, mysterious half-lights this was a hard row to hoe. Ten of Debussy's academic exercises have survived: five harmony exercises and five fugues. They contain nothing remarkable, although ironically, after Debussy's unflattering comment to Madame von Meck about Massenet's fugal abilities, in the preliminary rounds for both the 1883 and 1884 Prix de Rome competitions he found himself faced with fugue subjects by that gentleman.

Of more interest, if only in a negative sense, are his first two attempts at a Prix de Rome cantata. Guiraud seems to have felt that Debussy needed to devote the year 1881 to less taxing efforts, but in early 1882 Debussy tried his hand experimentally at a cantata text, *Daniel*, which had been set in 1868. The autograph fragments of this setting are currently inaccessible in private collections, but we can gauge the tone of the text well enough from the first line of the aria given to Balthazar, king of Assyria: 'Versez, que de l'ivresse/Aux accents d'allégresse / Circulent les doux feux!' (literally: Pour the wine, so that the gentle flames of intoxication may circulate with accents of joyfulness). No, *not* Banville.

In 1883 Guiraud allowed Debussy to enter for the *concours*. The text of the cantata *Le gladiateur* begins with the cry 'Death to the Romans!' and continues from there. That Debussy should have won second prize, as runner-up to Paul Vidal, says a good deal for his capacity to dissimulate, which has already been evident in his dealings with Madame von Meck. His brass writing in the 'March of the Gladiators', based on a rumpty-tumpty rhythm, is suitably banal and one of the few individual touches comes in the last three bars where the hero and heroine die in each other's arms, at which point Debussy marks the score 'morendo'. *In extremis*, he could usually muster a sense of humour.[9] But his feelings about the whole business became clear when the Vasniers came to see him in the courtyard one evening and the daughter, Marguerite, asked him why the windows had metal bars over them. 'No doubt,' he replied, 'because they regard us as wild animals.'

By the summer of 1884 Debussy had acquired a reputation in the Conservatoire, if not as a wild animal, then as a misfit and a trouble-maker. At the slightest opportunity, he would go to the keyboard and produce strings of dissonances, or else imitations of the horse-drawn buses rattling along the street outside. The scene at the public audition of the cantatas on the text of *L'enfant prodigue* (The Prodigal Son) on 27 June 1884 is described by his fellow pupil, Maurice Emmanuel:

> Nearly all of us had managed to get into the sanctuary. When Claude-Achille's turn came, and the air was filled with the opening chords of *L'enfant prodigue*, we exchanged delighted glances. But these soon faded. Instead of the scandal we were counting on, and despite occasional signs of agitation on the part of one or two elderly conductors who looked surprised and inclined to protest, compared with the outrageous harmonies which Debussy had served up to us previously, Claude-Achille's cantata struck us as debonair! It triumphed, in spite of some opposition. And while we did not grudge its success, we felt seriously let down that the expected brouhaha had not materialized.

The official verdict on Debussy's effort was 'a very definite sense of poetry, brilliant, warm colouring, lively, dramatic music' – and the positioning of French adjectives (*musique vivante et dramatique*) laid final emphasis on the quality that mattered to the judges above all. We may also note that Debussy had found two first-class singers for the roles of Azaël and Lia, the prodigal son and his mother: Ernest van Dyck had sung the role of Tristan in a concert version of Act I the previous March and was to sing other Wagnerian roles all over Europe in the following decades; Rose Caron had sung the role of Brunehilde in the premiere of Reyer's *Sigurd* at the Théâtre de la Monnaie in Brussels the previous January, and went on to sing Elsa and Desdemona in the Opéra premieres of *Lohengrin* (with van Dyck) and of *Otello*, in 1891 and 1894. Debussy may have suffered from an unpractical dreaminess in some areas of his life, but there were to be no 'artifices of negligence' when it came to arranging performances of his music.

This success meant that Debussy was to leave Paris in early 1885 and spend at least the next two years in Rome. In a newspaper article in June 1903, having categorised the Prix de Rome as 'a game, or rather a national sport', he looked back to that day of his success:

I was waiting on the pont des Arts for the results of the *concours*, watching the delightful patterns made by the *bateaux-mouches* on the Seine . . . Suddenly someone tapped me on the shoulder and said, breathlessly: 'You've won the prize!' Believe it or not, I can assure you my heart sank! I saw clearly the irritations and worries the smallest official position brings in its train. What's more, I realized I was no longer free.

'. . . que je n'étais plus libre.' As to irritations and worries, had Debussy been more prescient, he might rather have exclaimed over those that would descend on him thanks to this very craving for 'liberté'.

The seven months between winning the Prix de Rome and setting off for the Eternal City were not particularly happy ones for him. As Mme von Meck had noted, he was essentially a Parisian and from now on would leave the city only for the occasional holiday, to conduct his works (and make money) or to please his wife of the time. Everyone was busy telling him what a wonderful place Rome was and how lucky etc., etc. With his natural inclination to rebel against conformity he seems to have been determined that he was not going to enjoy his stay in Rome. For one thing, he would be parting from Mme Vasnier. For another, in the Villa Medici he would be removed from the intellectual life of Paris.

A detailed portrait of Debussy at this time is painted in a letter written in July 1884 by his fellow student Paul Vidal to Henriette Fuchs. Mme Fuchs ran a choral society called La Concordia for which Vidal had acted as accompanist until he left for Rome, having triumphed with his version of *Le gladiateur* in 1883. He recommended Debussy to Mme Fuchs as a replacement, a duty on which Debussy duly embarked. An article Mme Fuchs wrote in 1885 in *La revue chrétienne* made it clear this was not just any old choral society. There was a strong Protestant input, concerts were in general to be given for charitable purposes and she hoped that La Concordia would be an example in the creation of 'amateur societies belonging to the cultivated classes'. Vidal's somewhat agonized letter, which is worth quoting at length, needs to be read in this context:

So our friend Achille has won the prize despite himself! This sinister tale of adultery has been played out over a long period. Last year I had to persuade him to compete in the final round, against his wishes. Then during the winter he told me he wouldn't leave for Rome even if he won, that he was prevented from doing so. I can't say I was surprised, but even so I was angry for the moment and sorry I'd put him forward as accompanist for La Concordia . . .

He's incapable of any sacrifice. Nothing has any hold over him. His parents aren't rich, but instead of using the money from his teaching to support them, he buys new books for himself, knicknacks, etchings etc. His mother has shown me drawers full of them . . . His father has found it practically impossible to forgive the abandonment of the lucrative virtuoso career he'd dreamt of and has only just begun to recognize him as a composer, and that only from the time he started winning prizes for it. His mother loves him too much, she wants him with her all the time, wants to see him working hard etc., and that exasperates him. So his parents have no control over him. That leaves only Guiraud; he's always treated Debussy like a spoilt child and Debussy has paid him back by never turning up on time – I know, because he sometimes came to see me when he should have been at the class! But if anyone can influence him it's Guiraud.

His succubus is battening on to all his little weaknesses. She's pretty and much pursued by admirers, which pleases her jealous vanity; it appears she's a talented singer (I haven't heard her) and sings his songs extremely well; everything he writes is for her and owes its existence to her. How can one expect him in the circumstances to exile himself for two years in Rome, which he already knows and abhors! . . .

I thought for a moment, last year, that art had recovered its hold over him; which was why, wanting him to succeed, I introduced him to you and warmly supported his appointment with La Concordia. But his present behaviour fills me with remorse. Massenet won't find it easy to pardon the support I've given him, if he ever does! I've betrayed the flag to no good purpose and truly I'm sorry to have got mixed up in it all, and not to have let things take their course. His moral sense is undeveloped, he's nothing but a sensualist. I'm furious. I've acted like an imbecile. But, with all that, he has such talent and such a personality!

What can I possibly write to him? Rome is intolerable, life in the Villa is odious, there's no stimulus to compose anything . . . His is not a responsive character, he won't be able to benefit from the several good fellows there are here, I feel really powerless . . .
To think I love an animal who doesn't love his mother!

Before we follow Debussy on his journey to Rome, there are at least half a dozen points in this fascinating letter which may be examined with profit. First, the reference to Debussy teaching. With the Prix de Rome under his belt, he would have had no difficulty finding pupils, but it is symptomatic of his attitude to the profession that he never mentions what was probably his financial lifeline. Then there's Guiraud and the strength of his influence. Unwilling though Vidal may be to admit it, or to suggest it to Mme Fuchs's Protestant conscience, it may have been only through a tolerance and sympathy bordering on the complaisant that Guiraud was able to maintain any useful contact with Debussy whatever. To drive Debussy was to drive him away. He obviously did not thrive in the Concordia atmosphere, since he was always making excuses for absence and when, in 1887, Mme Fuchs's husband at a dinner proposed a vote of thanks to the society's accompanists, Vidal and Debussy's successor Charles René were mentioned, but not the errant Achille.[10]

A third point is that Vidal refers to Mme Vasnier as Debussy's 'succubus'. Obviously in such a milieu this relationship was a cause for scandal, but Vidal indicates firmly enough that she was no helpless victim of a callow passion. He was near enough right, too, in saying that everything Debussy wrote 'is for her and owes its existence to her': witness the dedications on several of the songs he wrote for her – 'to Mme Vasnier, the only muse who has ever inspired in me anything resembling a musical feeling (not to mention anything else)' and, on the volume of songs he presented to her, 'to Mme Vasnier, these songs which have come to life through her alone, and which will lose their enchanting gracefulness if they nevermore pass her melodious fairy lips'.

On this evidence, Vidal may seem to be near the mark in saying that Debussy's moral sense was undeveloped. But to call him 'nothing but a sensualist' was to ignore the contribution his sensuality made to his music, as well as the technique required to incorporate that sensuality into his current musical language. In the early songs, this sensuality is grafted for the most part on a style borrowed from Massenet. But in the second of the thirteen songs in what is now known as 'the Vasnier songbook' Debussy progressed unmistakably towards what would become his own language of love. Completed on 16 September 1882, his first setting of 'En sourdine' was far from being chronologically the last song in the collection, but it was the only one whose text combined a description of two lovers in each other's arms with the authorship of Paul Verlaine. Not that Debussy had finished with Banville, as we shall see in the next chapter, but Verlaine provided him both with a rich sensuality of language and with a crucial atmosphere of 'apartness', to be found in another medium in the love duet of *Tristan*. From the very first bar, the song is clearly describing a mystery, almost a religious experience. As often with early Debussy, the tone is not wholly consistent throughout, but the intention can hardly be misinterpreted.

Two last points from Vidal's letter concern two institutions of different kinds: Massenet and Rome. It is noticeable that, although Massenet was a composition professor at the Conservatoire from 1878 until 1896 – that is, through the last six years of Debussy's career there – there is no mention in Debussy's writings of him as a person, only of his music. And here Debussy's feelings were patently confused. Grudging praise alternates with savage criticism. In a letter to André Poniatowski of February 1893 he fulminated, 'we've just had a *Werther* by Massenet, displaying an extraordinary talent for satisfying every kind of stupidity and the poetic and operatic needs of cheap dilettantes!' And yet on Massenet's death in 1912 he took the trouble to write a tribute in *Le matin* of 14 August. Here, after assuring his readers that 'Massenet was the most truly loved of contemporary composers', he noted that whereas young milliners never hummed bits of the *Saint Matthew Passion*, they were well known to wake up singing *Manon* and *Werther*; and that this was a legitimate source of envy among the purists. I suspect he had throughout his life a sneaking regard for Massenet's music, but felt that, as with Wagner's, the doses had to be carefully prescribed. On Massenet's side, quite why, according to Vidal, he should object to his supporting Debussy must remain in the realm of conjecture.

Finally, Vidal's sour remarks about Rome and the Villa discount to some extent the notion that Debussy's reluctance to take up residence was due entirely to the pangs of love and to a childish, unreasoning affection for his native city. If I, Vidal, find the place lacking in stimulus, he seems to be saying, how much more will Debussy suffer, seeing what another kind of stimulus has produced over the last three years? A look at Debussy's list of works perhaps tells its own story. If the latest chronology is correct, during those seven months between winning the prize in June 1884 and travelling to Rome at the end of the following January, Debussy may well have composed nothing except an unfinished submission for a prize awarded by the city of Paris (or was this unnamed piece, mentioned only in a letter to Mme Fuchs, just an excuse for missing rehearsals?), some passages added to a project dating from three years earlier, and one song, 'L'ombre des arbres'. The words are by Verlaine; it is not dedicated to Mme Vasnier. It is tempting to read more of Debussy's feelings than is perhaps warranted into the superscription from Cyrano de Bergerac: 'the nightingale on a high branch, seeing himself reflected in the water, thinks he has fallen into the river. He is at the very top of an oak tree and yet he is afraid of drowning.'

2   Roman holiday? (1885–1887)

Debussy took the train to Rome, arriving there on Friday 30 January 1885, just a day before the latest date stipulated by the regulations.

In his reminiscences published in *Gil Blas* nearly twenty years later, he seized on a few salient points of his stay at the Villa Medici that he thought would make entertaining copy. Louis Cabat, the director of the Villa when Debussy arrived, was succeeded that June by the painter Ernest Hébert. Debussy recalled that

> his intolerance concerning everything to do with Rome and the Villa Medici has remained proverbial . . . He permitted no criticism of those two subjects. I remember complaining about the green walls of my bedroom which seemed to recede as you walked towards them – the room is famous among the inmates as the 'Etruscan Tomb'. M. Hébert insisted this was of no importance. He even went so far as to say that, if necessary, you could sleep in the ruins of the Coliseum . . . The benefits of experiencing a 'historical frisson' would compensate for the risk of catching a fever.

Debussy goes on to remember that Hébert, though a music lover, could not stand Wagner; unlike the young Debussy who was 'a Wagnerian to the point of forgetting the most basic rules of politeness'. In the first instance, his knowledge of Wagner must have come from excerpts (what Ernest Newman was to call 'bleeding chunks') in Paris orchestral concerts, especially those conducted by Charles Lamoureux, or from reading the scores, at which Debussy was

2 Debussy in Rome, 1885

remarkably adept. There was no stage performance in Paris of a
Wagner opera between the *Tannhäuser* fiasco of 1861 and the production of *Lohengrin* at the Eden-Théâtre in April 1887, a month after
Debussy's final return from Rome to Paris. But the recent researches
of François Lesure have established that he could have seen *Lohengrin*
before then, at the Apollo Theatre in Rome in the first fortnight after
his arrival.

The two most important criticisms of the Villa that Debussy makes
in his 1903 article are, nonetheless, that interaction with Roman society is practically non-existent, and that the students are plunged into a
new-found artistic freedom which they are quite unable to cope with.

'It is not the students' fault', he goes on, 'if their aesthetic stance is a little unsteady; it is the fault of those who send them off to a country where everything speaks to them of art at its purest, but who then leave them free to interpret this art in their own way.'

Either the students lose their liberty, as Debussy feared on the Pont des Arts, or they have too much . . . The answer to this conundrum was, I feel, that Debussy would have much preferred to enjoy his liberty in Paris, where he would have had a better idea what to do with it. Although he did somehow manage to snatch a few days in Paris in April and visited the Vasnier family (but not his parents), the events he missed out on there in 1885 included the first performance in the city of *Rigoletto*, the premieres of Reyer's *Sigurd* and Massenet's *Le cid* and the first performances of Franck's *Les djinns* and Chabrier's *La sulamite*; also Victor Hugo's imposing state funeral, not to mention the excitement surrounding the move of the night-club Le chat noir from the boulevard Rochechouart to larger premises on the rue Victor Massé. None of these would necessarily have had any direct influence on his music (certainly not *Rigoletto*), but at least they would have served as stimuli – to his wit, his enthusiasm or his distaste – and would have confirmed this 'gamin parisien' in that most necessary of feelings, that of being in the swim.

Regular journeys back to Paris were clearly not an option, for financial reasons apart from any reluctance on the part of M. Hébert – a chronically absconding student would hardly promote his preferred message that all things Roman were wonderful. The best Debussy could do was to keep abreast of the latest French novels and poetry, and this he did through friends (the poet Bourget sending him some of his latest work) and later through the Paris bookseller Emile Baron who supplied him with, among other things, books by Moréas and Huysmans, a play by Dumas *fils* and a translation of Shelley. Vidal later remembered how Debussy was also thrilled by the *Déliquescences* published by a pseudonymous Adoré Floupette, in which meaning comes a poor second to sound.

All the students at the Villa Medici, painters, architects, sculptors, engravers and musicians, had to produce an *envoi* at the end of each year to prove to the authorities of the Institut that they had not been wasting their time. For the musicians this was expected to take the form of a substantial orchestral or choral-and-orchestral piece. Beyond that no rules were laid down so that the exercise became, in some sense, a matter of knowing your jury: in this case, the six composers filling the designated chairs in the Académie des Beaux-Arts which formed one of the five sections of the Institut. In 1885 these included Ambroise Thomas, Gounod, Massenet and Saint-Saëns. Difficulties in guessing the collective mind of such a body were compounded by the fact that the members did not always see eye to eye. When, for example, Massenet was elected in 1878, he had immediately sent a telegram to his unsuccessful rival Saint-Saëns saying, 'The Institut has just committed a great injustice.' Saint-Saëns's return telegram simply read, 'I agree.'

No student, let alone one working as far away as Rome, could possibly expect to be *au fait* with the internal politics of such a group. Two best courses of action would seem to have commended themselves: either to aim your *envoi*, as it were, at what you considered to be the centre of the group; or else to write simply to please yourself. Dissembling may have won Debussy the Rome prize in the first place. But it is not hard to guess which of the two policies would be Debussy's, now that the prize was his.

It has always been easy to criticise the set-up at the Villa Medici and such criticism built up over the years until the Prix de Rome was finally abolished in 1968. Nowadays, no good educational institution would allow a student to pass from one system where he attended classes at least twice a week, to one where he had effectively no supervision whatever and had to produce one large work at the end of a year or more. And yet Debussy took his responsibilities very seriously, for all his grumbling.

The story of his struggles with the first *envoi* is told largely in his letters to Mme Vasnier's husband, Eugène. Whether he was complaisant in Debussy's affair with his wife or merely ignorant of it, we cannot now tell. At all events he was obviously a kind friend to the young composer during these difficult times, to judge from Debussy's replies which, after the routine apology for tardiness, regularly acknowledge M. Vasnier's encouragement to stay in Rome and see the thing through. On 4 June, four months after his arrival, he wrote to M. Vasnier, complaining that he had had a bad attack of fever, but then explaining his composing plans:

> I've changed my mind about my first *envoi*. *Zuléima* is not the right sort of thing at all, so I shan't be going ahead with it as I intended. It's too old and too stuffy. Those great stupid lines bore me to death – the only thing great about them is their length – and my music would be in danger of sinking under the weight. Another thing, and more important, is that I don't think I shall ever be able to cast my music in a rigid mould . . . I would always rather deal with something where the passage of events is to some extent subordinated to a thorough and extended portrayal of human feelings. That way, I think, music can become more personal, more true to life; you can explore and refine your means of expression.

The remark about 'the passage of events' (*l'action*) may be taken as showing Debussy's disenchantment with the plot-led tendencies in contemporary opera. An extreme point was reached over the next couple of years with Emmanuel Chabrier's *Le roi malgré lui*, in which some superb music was hobbled by a ridiculously complex story full, as Vincent d'Indy said, of 'people arriving when they ought to leave, and leaving when they ought to stay where they are'. It argues an extraordinary grasp of principles in a twenty-two-year-old to have understood that this system, which in a less extreme form had served opera reasonably well throughout the nineteenth century, was not for him: that instead of lavish scenery, choral set pieces and what Wagner castigated in French grand opera as 'effects without causes', the ingredients of opera could be both subtle and intimate.

The 'great stupid lines' of *Zuléima* had been concocted by one Georges Boyer, based on Heine's *Almansor*. According to Edward Lockspeiser, 'in this drama, dealing with the persecution of Moors in

Spain, the Moorish beauty Zuleima, converted to Christianity, is betrothed to a Christian knight. Almansor ben Abdullah, determined to win Zuleima, carries her off on his horse, but his Christian enemies overtake them and, dismounting from their horse, the couple plunge to their death in a ravine.'[1] All of which did not leave much time for a 'thorough and extended portrayal of human feelings'. But once Debussy had decided to remain true to himself rather than toe this party line (which he later confessed smacked of Verdi and Meyerbeer), his thoughts reverted to a work he had been tinkering with, on and off, for five years: a 'comédie héroïque' called *Diane au bois* by Théodore de Banville.

Among the most recent Debussy autographs to be rediscovered is one for piano duet marked 'Diane. Ouverture.' It is dated 'Rome 1881'. This in itself is confusing because, although Debussy did visit Rome with the von Mecks, that was in 1880 and not 1881, when they stayed in Russia. That aside, the music is best left in obscurity: the material is undistinguished and it shows a predilection for repeating everything which soon palls. Altogether more interesting are the pages which have been known for some years, of Debussy's setting of the duet between Eros and Diana from Act II of Banville's drama.

It is possible that this is the music which Debussy brought to Guiraud's class shortly before going in for the Prix de Rome in the summer of 1884 – on which Guiraud's advice was, 'If you want to win the prize, dear boy, leave that sort of thing till afterwards.' Even in the first dozen bars, in which we find the flute/horn ambience that was to haunt the next decade, there are dissonances that do indeed look ahead to Debussy's later music, specifically to the opening of 'Jeux de vagues' in *La mer* of 1905, and even to that of Vaughan Williams's Fifth Symphony of 1943. On this evidence Guiraud's advice looks sound.

So although Debussy was going back in a chronological sense, he was really only trying to complete unfinished business which might provide a springboard for the future. His letter of 4 June explains his hopes for the new text:

Another reason for choosing *Diane* is that it's nothing at all like the usual poems set for *envois*, which are basically no more than improved cantatas. Heaven knows, one was enough! I may as well take advantage of the one good thing the Villa has to offer (as you said), complete freedom to work, in order to produce something original and not keep falling back into old habits . . . The nub of the matter is that my sort of music is the only sort I can write. Whether I shall be strong enough to do it is something I have yet to find out.

Debussy's doubts as to whether he would prove 'assez fort' suggest that he trusted neither to the traditional idea of inspiration nor to Baudelaire's claim that it was 'the sister of daily labour', but rather to some kind of internal, mental discipline: as his friend and pupil Raoul Bardac later remembered,

he was of the opinion that one should create slowly and with minute care the special atmosphere in which a work has to evolve; one should not rush to write things down, so as to allow complete freedom to those mysterious, inner workings of the mind which are too often stifled by impatience.

This discipline involved not only finding the good, but excluding the bad, the irrelevant or the derivative. On 19 October he wrote to M. Vasnier again:

As for *Diane*, one scene is finished, though I'm not at all happy with it – it's far from being right. Apart from anything else, it could be that I've taken on something too ambitious. There's no precedent to go on and I find myself compelled to invent new forms. I could always turn to Wagner, but I don't need to tell you how ridiculous it would be even to try. The only thing of his I would want to copy is the running of one scene into another. Also I want to keep the tone lyrical without its being absorbed by the orchestra.

Five weeks later, on 24 November, another letter proves how right he had been to talk of needing to be strong:

Diane is giving me a lot of trouble. I can't manage to find a musical idea that gives me the look of her, as I imagine it. In fact it's quite difficult, because the idea must be beautiful but cold – it mustn't give any hint of passion. Love comes to Diane only much later and then it's only really by accident; I'll have to get it across through the transformation of this idea, step by step, as Diane loses her resistance to love, but the idea must keep the same contour throughout.

To proceed through transformation of a thematic idea and yet keep out of Wagner's clutches – this was ambition indeed. The heart of Debussy's efforts was this attempt to focus on what was essential. The orchestra was not to be used to help him out of difficulties with the vocal line nor was depth of insight to be confused with complication of texture. Eileen Souffrin has noted[2] that 'the cuts Debussy makes in Banville's text have the result of suppressing the secondary characters. Systematically he removes the nymphs who, in the play, keep us abreast of the action. In the extant manuscript, Debussy picks up Banville's text at the point where the two main characters come together: plainly it is the conflict between Eros and Diana which excites his interest.'

Mme Souffrin further suggests that in the story of the passionate Eros attempting to win the cold Diana Debussy read something of his own situation vis-à-vis Marie Vasnier. This is possible. If so, the sensation of discussing with a cuckolded husband the aesthetic bases of a story which mirrored his own cuckolding must have been a strange one, but not on that account to be ruled out. Debussy, like the rest of cultured France, had read Huysmans's novel *A rebours*, published the previous year, in which at one point the hero Des Esseintes has recourse to fear as a way of stimulating his jaded passion. Debussy's determination 'to be original and not keep falling back into old habits' was itself a guarantee of living and working, if not exactly in fear, then at least dangerously.

In the event, *Diane au bois* was to prove too hard a task at this stage of his career. He soldiered on with it through the early months of 1886 but in the end, after a brief flirtation with a piece based on Flaubert's *Salammbô*, he returned for his first *envoi* to *Zuléima*, great stupid lines and all. The score is lost, and the chances are that Debussy destroyed it when it was returned to him from the Institut after its first and probably only performance in December 1886. If we are to believe his own statement of October 1885 that the music was pseudo-Verdi combined with pseudo-Meyerbeer, then the judges' only complaint, one would have thought, might be that it was insufficiently French – though of course we have no way of knowing what changes Debussy may have made before he finally submitted it. But this was not the burden of their song when their opinion was published in the *Journal officiel* on 31 December 1886:

> M. Debussy currently seems to be tormented by the desire to write music that is bizarre, incomprehensible and unperformable. Despite certain passages which are not without a certain character, the vocal lines of his work are of no interest either from the melodic point of view or from that of his use of words (*la déclamation*).

Debussy may well have ignored these comments and put the whole unpleasant business behind him. For us, it is a pity that the music has not survived so that we could ourselves judge how this music could be simultaneously bizarre and dull. After all, his grasp of *déclamation* (which means not only word-setting in the sense of the manipulation of stress and syllable-length, but also the way in which the setting matches the psychological import of the words) had been approved in *L'enfant prodigue*. What new paths had he chosen to explore?

We may briefly look at the social context in which these compositional struggles took place. Some later memoirs of Achille at the Villa were to portray him as an unsocial being, and these have often been seized upon with ill-concealed glee by less sympathetic commentators. Gabriel Pierné, for instance, the 1882 prizewinner, was still in Rome when Debussy arrived. 'Although he lived side by side with his fellow students', Pierné wrote in 1926, 'there was no real intimacy between them. He went out a lot, spent his time with antique dealers and made a clean sweep of tiny Japanese objects which entranced him. He was never to be seen except at meals.'

Most of this is simply not true. We have to accept that from his earliest years Debussy had a talent for upsetting those close to him, and indeed he was to confess later in life to being a bit of a grump ('je suis un ours' – literally, 'I'm a bear'), but in his younger days he could, when he chose, be the life and soul of the party. It seems as if he may have found Pierné a bit stuffy; in 1911 he described his conducting of La mer as 'awful and frustrating' and three years later wrote to him to say that in rehearsal Jeux had by and large been too loud. Nor should we be misled by the fact that in that letter he addresses Pierné as 'tu' into thinking that there was any close rapport between them: by convention, all students at the Villa addressed each other in this way and naturally the habit persisted into later life. A quite different view of Debussy the student comes from two other sources: Paul Vidal and Mme Hébert, the director's wife.

According to Vidal, he, Debussy and Xavier Leroux, who had won the 1885 prize with the cantata Endymion, formed an 'inseparable trio' from the time Leroux arrived and Pierné departed, in January 1886. 'The afternoons would be spent', he wrote, 'in sightreading Bach's organ works, with each of us taking turns to play the pedal part. In the evening, we would meet in Debussy's room and declaim the plays of Shakespeare or Banville.'[3] According to Vidal, Debussy was not 'the solitary figure he liked to portray in his correspondence', which looks perhaps to have been a ploy to prepare M. Vasnier for his early return to Paris, should this come about for whatever reason. Or perhaps the mask of the lonely misfit, once put on, was embarrassing to lay aside?

Incontrovertible evidence that Debussy was indeed involved in the social life of the Villa comes from Mme Hébert's diary.[4] On 20 June 1885, less than a fortnight after Hébert's arrival as the new director, they and a mutual friend, Count Primoli, took Debussy out in their carriage to the Borghese Gardens, followed by dinner and a recital by Debussy of some of his Bourget settings ('Paysage sentimental' seems to have been a general favourite). Half a dozen further dinners and outings took place over the next ten days or so, leading Debussy to complain that the Héberts' kindness was making his life a misery. He managed to arrange a two-month leave of absence from early July on some pretext to do with his health, but in fact to go and stay with the Vasniers in Dieppe. The Héberts, who were fully aware of his liaison with Marie Vasnier, may have felt, as Guiraud had done, that Debussy was likely to react badly to direct resistance and that tolerance was the best course.

Shortly after Debussy's return on 2 September, the Héberts went on leave until the end of the year, and the Villa's social life resumed only in January 1886. But in the meantime, as Debussy recounted in a letter of 24 November to M. Vasnier, he underwent an important musical experience:

> I went to hear two masses, one by Palestrina, the other by Orlando de Lassus, in a church called the Anima [Santa Maria dell'Anima] . . . It's very simple and pure in style, quite different from so many of the others . . . The Anima is certainly the right place to hear that kind of music, the only church music I regard as legitimate. That of Gounod & Co. strikes me as the product of hysterical mysticism – it's like a sinister practical joke.
>
> The two above-named gentlemen are true masters, especially Orlando, who is more decorative, more human than Palestrina. I'm truly amazed at the effects they can get simply from a vast knowledge of counterpoint. I expect you think of counterpoint as the most forbidding article in the whole of music. But in their hands it becomes something wonderful, adding an extraordinary depth to the meaning of the words. And every now and then the melodic lines unroll and expand, reminding you of the illuminations in ancient missals. And those are the only occasions when my real musical self has given a slight stir.

This is the same letter in which Debussy speaks of trying to compress the essence of Diane into a single phrase and there can be little doubt that Lassus and Palestrina showed him a possible way of harnessing economical methods to produce stirring effects. At the same time he was quick to realize their 'vast knowledge of counterpoint' (*une science énorme de contrepoint*) which alone made their approach valid, and which he, after just a few years of writing fugues for four voices, simply did not possess. This single visit to the Church of Santa Maria dell'Anima may well have been one of the two most influential events of his time in Rome.

The other was indisputably Liszt's arrival in Rome on 5 January 1886, preceded by a prescription of his dietary needs sent to the Villa by Princess Sayn-Wittgenstein. On the 8th, after dinner, Debussy and Vidal played him a piano duet arrangement of his *Faust Symphony* (during which the *maître* went to sleep), and probably it was next day that they played him Chabrier's *Trois valses romantiques*, at that time barely two years old; we do not know of Liszt's reaction (at least he seems to have stayed awake), but the appeal to Debussy of these pieces is easy to understand when we read of Chabrier's own insistence that they should *not* be played as though written by a member of the Institut!

Shortly after this, the atmosphere of the Villa was enlivened by the visit of M. and Mme Hochon, especially by that of the attractive Loulou. Not that any whiff of this comes through from Debussy's account to M. Vasnier in his letter of 29 January:

> The Villa is currently very full as Hébert brought some guests back with him. A Monsieur Hochon has also arrived. They're all, it seems, very sophisticated people – I don't know if you're acquainted with them. I've met them once and they were full of kind wishes sent by Guiraud. But all that's neither here nor there and does absolutely nothing to make me love the Villa more. Luckily I've found a way to get myself out of boring social occasions: I told Hébert I'd sold my evening dress and that my financial resources did not permit me to have another suit made. He thought I was mad, but who cares? I got what I wanted because he's too much of a decorum-worshipper to allow a mere lounge-suit to appear amid the splendour of *décolleté* gowns and tail-coats.

Whether we are to believe that or not, 11 days later, on 9 February, Mme Hébert wrote (in English) in her diary that Count Primoli 'tells me that they have seen Loulou and Debussy kissing in the Villa'. As

François Lesure notes, 'the manuscript of "Green" (from Verlaine's *Ariettes*) is dated precisely from this January and it is tempting to think that these "final kisses", "this heart that beats only for you" perhaps no longer referred to the lady far away in Paris . . .'5

From the lack of any mention of her in Debussy's correspondence we may judge that Marie Vasnier was indeed no longer at the centre of his thoughts. He took two months official holiday in June and July in Paris – whether he visited the Vasniers, we do not know – before returning for what was to be his final eight months' stint in Rome. Evidence for his activities over this period is scanty. Between 11 November and 25 February 1887 the Héberts entertained him no fewer than fourteen times, though Mme Hébert's only memorable entry is to the effect that on the evening of 11 February 'Debussy delighted Mme de Pourtalès' (the Countess Mélanie de Pourtalès). During this time Debussy was also coming to the decision that he could no longer bear to stay in Rome. On 24 February he broke his long silence towards M. Vasnier by telling him of his plans:

> I know what would happen to me if I stayed – total obliteration. Ever since I've been here I've felt dead inside. I really want to work, and go on till I produce something solid and original. And another thing – you know how I always get serious doubts when I'm working; I need someone whose judgement I can rely on to reassure me. That's what I found so often in you – you gave me courage. Whenever you approved of something I'd written I used to feel stronger. There's no chance of that here. My fellow students make fun of my misery and I needn't look for encouragement from that quarter.

Or was the truth rather, as Debussy confided to his bookseller friend Emile Baron, that he felt the need to see some Monets and hear some Offenbach? The last mention of him in Mme Hébert's diary is dated 2 March: 'I put together provisions for Debussy. He leaves this evening . . . [He] doesn't give me *Paysage sentimental* nor does he pay off any of his debts.'

In the financial sense, this was probably true. But Debussy was careful enough of his official position to see to it that his debt to the

Institut, in the shape of his second *envoi*, was at least partly paid by the
deadline of the end of February. On the 9th he wrote to Baron that
'compared with mine, a convict's life is one of irresponsible ease and
luxury'. Even so, he did not manage to complete the *envoi* on time, so
he invented the story that the score of *Printemps* had been burnt at the
binder's. The Institut received only an orchestral sketch with 'a few
pages reorchestrated in haste': this sketch is presumably the autograph for chorus and two pianos now in the Library of Texas at Austin,
dated 23 February 1887.

We should remember that only a couple of months had passed
since the Institut had savaged his first *envoi*, *Zuléima*. Debussy might,
as I have suggested, simply have put this behind him as being of no
account, but it still left the problem of what to offer them for the
future. In this context, it is instructive to read what he wrote to Baron
on 9 February, four weeks before leaving the Villa for Paris:

> I've decided to write a work of a special colour, recreating as many
> sensations as possible. I'm calling it *Printemps*, not 'spring' from the
> descriptive point of view but from that of living things. I wanted to
> express the slow, laborious birth of beings and things in nature, then
> the mounting florescence, and finally a burst of joy at being reborn
> to a new life, as it were.
>
> There's no detailed programme, of course, as I have nothing but
> contempt for music organized according to one of those leaflets
> they're so careful to provide you with as you come into the concert
> hall. I'm sure you see how powerful and evocative the music needs
> to be, and I'm not sure I shall be wholly successful in this.

Once again, after meeting the Establishment on its own terms in
winning the Prix de Rome, Debussy was determined, as with *Diane au
bois* and probably with *Zuléima* as well, to use the 'freedom' of Rome to
write his own music – in modern parlance, to 'go for it'.

Since 1887, spring has continued to be celebrated in music, for
example in such differing works as Stravinsky's *Le sacre du printemps*, in
which the composer recalled 'the violent Russian spring that seemed
to begin in an hour and was like the whole earth cracking',[6] and in

Britten's Spring Symphony, in which the composer, using language almost identical with Debussy's, aimed to portray 'the progress from winter to spring and the reawakening of the earth and life which that means'.[7] For all the difference in musical language between Debussy, Stravinsky and Britten, and for all that Le sacre contains a cruel, sacrificial element missing from the other two works, all three celebrate the miracle of reviving life and its apparent fragility during 'the very dead of winter'.

The form in which Debussy's Printemps was published, in an orchestration by Henri Busser made in 1912 under the composer's eye, means that we must be careful about committing ourselves to historical judgements. Even so, we can reasonably assume that the opening unaccompanied pentatonic phrase was part of his original conception – a naive, 'natural' idea, as it were the seed of life beneath the hard crust of silence. And it is tempting to identify this cautious entry into the world of sound with Debussy's own predicament as a composer. As he said, his own kind of music was the only music he knew how to write. But not only was this kind of music regarded as bizarre and incomprehensible by the Establishment, there were also the far more serious problems that lay within himself, notably the gap he was forced to acknowledge between his aims and his technique for realizing them. As James Hepokoski has noted, there is a family of Debussy openings that act as vestibules or initiation rites, apparently preparing the listener to enter a temple or some religious ceremony.[8] One could relate this to some nascent religious feeling in the composer, perhaps provoked by hearing Palestrina and Lassus, and ignore Debussy's later protestations of atheism. Alternatively, and less ambitiously, one could suggest that he was merely obeying a compulsion to tread warily on the new path he was simultaneously hacking through the musical undergrowth. It was a straight and narrow path, even a tidy one. As his friend Charles Koechlin wrote: 'Debussy loathed approximation (l'à peu près) and disorder. But order, in music, can be achieved in a thousand different ways and does not demand for its realization either dryness or scholasticism. It is as absurd to call one of Debussy's development passages amorphous as it is to classify a cat as an invertebrate because of its grace and suppleness.'[9] Also, cats look before they leap . . .

The published orchestral score of *Printemps* can give only a vague idea of Debussy's original intentions. On 7 March 1889, he wrote to Ernest Chausson:

> It's not a choral work (the chorus parts are *wordless* and treated more as an orchestral group). It's a symphonic suite *with chorus*. The interest therefore lies for the most part in the orchestra and the difficulty for the chorus consists in the idiosyncratic way (*la façon particulière*) in which they and the orchestra blend in together. The whole thing's a matter of ensemble and the mingling of colours; both need a light touch.

Whatever the correspondence between Debussy's ideal and the score for chorus and two pianos he submitted to the Institut, those worthies delivered their usual New Year present at the end of 1887 in the form of a report barely less scathing than the one on *Zuléima*, but a good deal more interesting for the modern reader. 'M. Debussy', they claimed,

> certainly does not err on the side of platitude or banality. He has, quite on the contrary, a too highly pronounced tendency to seek out what is strange. One can sense that he has a feeling for musical colour, but exaggeration of this easily leads him to forget the importance of precision of outline and clarity of form. It is devoutly to be wished that he be on his guard against that vague Impressionism which is one of the most dangerous enemies of truth in works of art.[10]

This was the first recorded mention of the word 'Impressionism' in connection with Debussy, though assuredly not the last. It was also one of the first uses of this painterly term in connection with music. We may assume that the six members of the music section of the Académie des Beaux-Arts from time to time discussed general artistic problems with their colleagues in the painters' section and it is certainly possible that these colleagues were encountering and deploring Impressionist tendencies in the *envois* they themselves were judging. If so, they were very close to the position of Renoir. The art historian Phoebe Pool records of Renoir that 'on a visit to Italy in 1881, the sight of the frescoes at Pompeii and those of Raphael made him realize that he was losing too much through the Impressionist abolition of shape and contour'.[11] Although the individual views of the music section were officially subsumed in the general report delivered by the secretary of the Académie, the story on the grapevine was that, while Gounod had tried to defend Debussy's score, Saint-Saëns had taken offence at the very opening bars, saying, 'One does not write for orchestra in six sharps.' Was it he especially who had noted these unpalatable Impressionist leanings, as he was to notice Cubist ones in *En blanc et noir* nearly thirty years later? What we do know is that, outliving Debussy by three years, he was able to mount a continuous and articulate campaign against his younger colleague, to which Debussy never deigned to respond, at least in public.

The paradox over *Printemps* is that Debussy was said to have been inspired, not by any daub of Renoir's or Pissarro's, but by a copy of Botticelli's *Primavera*, and also by the picture called *Printemps* based on it by his colleague at the Villa Marcel Baschet, who had just sent this back to Paris as his fourth *envoi*. Baschet's original has been destroyed, but Marcel Dietschy saw the sketch for it and described it as 'd'une grâce exquise' – which does not suggest any attempt at Impressionist boldness, but rather a faithful reflection of the original. So Debussy, with the sounds of Palestrina and Lassus in his ears, tries to recreate the atmosphere of Botticelli's masterpiece – and is taxed with dabbling in a technique that is 'an enemy to the truth'. Well might he, like Pontius Pilate, have asked, 'What is truth?'

There is, though, a pleasing symmetry in Debussy's arrival at the Villa and his leaving of it. He came to it, he said in a newspaper article in June 1903, 'not far from believing myself to be the little beloved of the gods described in ancient legends'. He left it having written a work based on Botticelli's *Primavera*, with the goddess Venus at its centre.

The picture had been painted in 1475 as an allusion to the reign of Lorenzo the Magnificent and the new era of youth and joy which he had inaugurated – what Debussy referred to in his letter to Baron of 9 February 1887 as 'une éclatante joie de renaître à une vie nouvelle'.

The question was: would Achille the Magnificent prove similarly to be the catalyst of a new era of youth and joy on his return to Paris?

3   A Bohemian in Paris (1887–1893)

Debussy's definitive return to Paris in early March 1887 should have been a happy one, if only because he was now no longer separated from Marie Vasnier. But, as her daughter Marguerite recalled in 1926,

> when he came back for good, the intimacy was no longer there. He had changed, as we had. We had moved house, made new friends, and he, with his moody, unsociable character and unwillingness to alter his habits, no longer felt at home ... He used to come, then, and ask for suggestions and advice, and even material help because, ... not yet having any sort of reputation, he still had to live.
>
> It was then that he put into practice the vague idea of giving me piano and harmony lessons, because he wanted to please my parents. What an appalling teacher! Not an ounce of patience and incapable of explaining anything in a way that could be understood by a young girl like myself; one had to have understood before he had finished explaining. We abandoned the enterprise ... Then gradually, he too made new acquaintances; he stopped coming and we never saw him again.[1]

His liaison with Marie did continue for a year or so and the painter Jacques-Emile Blanche caught sight of him climbing a rope ladder up to her window during a family holiday in Dieppe. But, as Marguerite says, his thoughts now were turned increasingly elsewhere, and particularly to the tiresome business of making a living – a knack he was never really to acquire.

His financial situation was not improved when, five weeks after his return, his father was made redundant from the Compagnie Fives-Lille. Since Achille was still living at home, the atmosphere must have been tense. Having completed his statutory two years in Rome (he did not leave prematurely, as has often been stated), he would still have been drawing the monthly allowance for Prix de Rome winners until March 1889, amounting to 167.50 francs a month. At a time when one franc would buy you quite a reasonable meal or *dinette* consisting of a plate of meat and one of vegetables, with cheese, wine and bread, these were not starvation wages. But of course they took no account of other necessaries such as heating and clothes, not to mention entertainment or Japanese knicknacks, and Debussy may also have felt obliged to give his mother something for his lodging.

The obvious answer – obvious, that is, for anyone who did not understand Debussy – was to take a regular teaching job, perhaps at some provincial conservatoire, or as a répétiteur in some provincial opera house; a Prix de Rome winner with a first prize in practical harmony, and no doubt a recommendation from the compliant Guiraud, would have had few problems finding such a post. Debussy seems never even to have considered anything of the sort. The piano lessons in the bourgeois households of Paris continued no doubt, but to a large extent Debussy was reliant on his friends, such as the Vasniers, for free meals and what Mlle Vasnier tactfully calls 'material aid' – that is, loans which, to judge from his past and future habits, would usually remain unreturned.

A fortnight after arriving in Paris he wrote Hébert a fairly long letter which, if we are to believe what he says rather than regarding it as a form of politeness towards his recent 'jailer', indicates that he faced the future with some misgivings:

> When I reached Paris, I felt like a little boy tentatively trying to make his way in the world (for Heaven's sake, I came near to being frightened by the carriages!). Even my friends struck me as people of substance. Vidal was very busy and grudgingly granted me lunch with him as a favour! Leroux permitted me an audience in the street

in between two appointments! As for Pierné . . . I don't even dare go and see him. All of them indeed treat Paris like a captured city! And you should see how compliant they are, how they have lost those fine feelings of indignation they used to harbour!

All of which irritated me slightly! And then, these last months in Rome have contributed to this state of mind; I have spent these months in a dream world, absorbed in my work, all my efforts directed towards a lofty artistic ideal, without bothering in the slightest as to what anyone else might think of it.

Now I'm wondering how, in my exaggeratedly uncultivated state, I shall find my way as I struggle in the midst of this 'success market', and I foresee innumerable anxieties and conflicts . . .

My best day so far was on Sunday at the Lamoureux Concert: the overture to [Reyer's] *Sigurd*: rather banal, rather the sort of music suitable for opening an industrial exhibition, with vulgar brass, muted strings, and an effect of overfamiliar melancholy, complete with part for the no less familiar 'nasal bassoon': fragments of *A Midsummer Night's Dream*: correct music! And finally, the first act of *Tristan and Isolde*: it is definitely the most beautiful music I know from the point of view of depth of emotion. It envelops you like a caress and makes you suffer; in short, you undergo the same emotions as Tristan, but without doing violence to your intellect or your heart. Not very well sung, but superbly played and at times even too accurately – one would like to see the music spring more freely. That's the only music I've heard, as the Opéra doesn't tempt me in the slightest.[2]

This fascinating letter repays closer study. Poor Gabriel Pierné now seems to have progressed in Debussy's eyes from a stuffy pedant to being the very embodiment of the Establishment composer, courted by publishers and played by the top Paris orchestras. And it was to get worse – three years later, at the age of twenty-seven, he succeeded César Franck as organist of Ste.-Clotilde. Anyone would think, from the way Debussy writes, that he too was aiming for such a position in Parisian musical life. But then he accuses Pierné and the others of being compliant (*souples*), effectively of selling out their musical gifts in order to make a name and a living, as distinct from himself who has been directing all his efforts 'towards a lofty artistic ideal'; and intends to go on doing so.

It is surely no accident that his talk of ideals is immediately offset by his twin experiences of banality and correctness in the works of Reyer and Mendelssohn, but then given sustenance by the first act of *Tristan*, 'definitely the most beautiful music I know from the point of view of depth of emotion'. He is even willing to sacrifice exactitude to the overall flow, wanting the music to 'spring more freely (*bondir plus librement*)'. *Bondir*, meaning to spring, leap, bounce, even to gambol, may seem an odd word to use of the first act of *Tristan*. But it suggests that what attracted Debussy to Wagner was not only his chromatic language but also the intense energy that his music can command. It is interesting too that he uses the word 'see' rather than 'hear': 'one would like to *see* the music . . .' This visual approach to an essentially aural art is typical of Debussy, who once admitted he was as happy looking at pictures as listening to music, and who on many occasions was prompted to compose by sights as well as sounds, and often by the two in combination. Though whether that necessarily makes him an Impressionist remains a matter for dispute.

The final point in that extract concerns the little appeal the Opéra repertoire had for him. The two directors at the time, Eugène Ritt and Pierre Gailhard, like all directors of the period, had a subsidy from the government but were free to put on whatever operas they liked, subject to just a few restrictions; and, if they managed to make a profit, it was theirs to keep. The usual balance had to be found between tried and tested favourites and new works which might, with luck, become favourites in their turn. Even that sometimes failed, when tried and tested works were tried and tested too thoroughly: in this same year of 1887, a subscriber complained to the directors that 'I shall not be subscribing again . . . Last winter, I swallowed twelve performances of [Paladilhe's] *Patrie* on Fridays, and I need a rest. When MM. Ritt and Gailhard feel like varying their repertoire a little, I shall resume the subscription I have been taking out for the last 20 years.'[3] It should, though, be pointed out that in the novelty stakes

1887 was a particularly bad year – one of only three years (1879, 1887 and 1889) when no Opéra premiere was given. The innovation of presenting *Faust* as the first Opéra matinée in February might be thought a poor substitute, while the same opera's 500th performance in November merely confirmed the worst. Overall though, the production of seventy-seven new works (new, that is, to the Opéra) in the thirty-nine years between 1875 and 1914 – effectively Debussy's opera-going lifetime – cannot fairly be seen as crassly unambitious, even if a fair number of them lasted only a season or two.

The centre of the Opéra repertoire consisted of some eleven operas: four by Meyerbeer (*Robert le diable*, *Les huguenots*, *Le prophète* and *L'africaine*), Halévy's *La juive*, Donizetti's *La favorite*, *Don Giovanni*, *Der Freischütz*, *William Tell*, *Faust* and Ambroise Thomas's *Hamlet*. Debussy later had admiring things to say about *Der Freischütz*, but none of the other operas drew his praise: he continued all his life to speak of Mozart as a master, but only in glosses on other topics – in none of his writings did he ever devote so much as a whole paragraph to Mozart, as he did, and more, to Bach, Rameau or Beethoven.

In a sense it is no surprise that any opera capable of filling the huge spaces of the Palais Garnier should by definition have failed to impress a composer who, as we have seen, aspired to an ideal of subtlety, delicacy and concentration. We must exclude Wagner from this company (*Lohengrin* in 1891 was the first of his operas to reach that stage, followed by others at regular intervals up to *Parsifal* in 1914); but then 'Wagner and Debussy' is a rather special case. Nor is it surprising that when Debussy for once abandoned some of his principles and set to work on a grand opera for this venue, his conscience prevented him from finishing it.

It was more natural for Debussy to look to the smaller Opéra-Comique for operas after his own heart – such as those of Offenbach who, as he wrote in a newspaper article in April 1903, 'by his gifts as an ironist was perhaps the only person to realize all that was false and inflated in [Meyerbeer's] art, and who above all was able to discover the secret hoard of extreme buffoonery this art contained and

exploited it – successfully, as we all know'. After eight years in purga-
tory, Carmen had been reinstated in 1883 and in the next eight years had
its revenge, notching up 400 performances on this stage – what
Debussy once referred to gleefully as 'the best box on the ears the critics have had'. As a Chabrier enthusiast, too, he would hardly have
missed the premiere of the badly plotted but musically delectable Le roi
malgré lui on 18 May 1887. What he did miss, luckily for him, was the
terrible fire at the Opéra-Comique which broke out a week later during
a double bill of Adam's one-act opera Le chalet and Thomas's Mignon.
Around eighty people were killed and the Opéra-Comique had to
move into temporary premises, initially into the Théâtre Lyrique in the
place du Châtelet.

All these operatic details are a necessary background, I think, to
understanding Debussy's position after his return to the capital. The
Opéra was irrelevant to his needs, the Opéra-Comique was temporar-
ily in turmoil. The Concerts Lamoureux were concentrating on
Wagner, the Concerts Colonne on Berlioz, Saint-Saëns and Bizet
(with novelties from Pierné). The Société nationale was his best
chance, and indeed several of his later works were to be performed at
its concerts. But for the moment this body too was in slight disarray,
following the coup of the previous year in which members of the bande
à Franck overturned the 'modern French music only' policy which had
obtained since the society's foundation in 1871, and won entry for foreign music and music of the past. There was therefore less room for
contemporary French works than hitherto.

This left the salons. Debussy would never see himself as a salon
animal – making small talk over the petits fours was his idea of forced
labour – but they did provide a ready market for piano music and
songs, with the possibility that an editor might hear them.
Debussy's reputation nowadays rests to a considerable extent on his
piano music. But, for whatever reason, he was slow to find his own
style in the medium and the Two Arabesques for instance, written
between 1888 and 1891, though charming and melodious, in no way
prefigure the revolution in piano writing Debussy was to help bring

about. It was in song writing that he took his first steps towards true individuality.

He had made five settings of Verlaine's poetry in 1882 and the early part of 1883. Then his interest had turned to the poems of Paul Bourget, together with one setting of Mallarmé ('Apparition') in 1884. His attraction to Bourget seems to have waned thereafter and, as we have seen, on the brink of his journey to Rome in January 1885 he returned to Verlaine and his poem 'L'ombre des arbres', with the nightingale watching its reflection in the river below. By 1887, and possibly by the end of March that year, he had completed another five songs on Verlaine texts and these were published in 1888.

Few would dispute that in these *Ariettes*, republished with a few changes as the collection *Ariettes oubliées* in 1903, Debussy rose to new heights. Although in their original form they were dedicated to Marie Vasnier, he had now put to one side any deference to her coloratura abilities and achieved an economy of language and an accuracy in painting mood that were to be hallmarks of his songs from now on. There is also a new sensuousness in a song such as 'C'est l'extase', which translates Verlaine's portrait of post-coital languor with such fidelity as to make its acceptance in respectable salons somewhat doubtful. Above all, he manages somehow to capture the sadness at the heart of much of the poetry: the rain in the poet's heart matching the rain that falls on the city; his fear that his beloved will leave him; and, in the vigorous 'Chevaux de bois', the melancholy that descends when a day at the fair has finally to come to an end. With almost unerring consistency he achieves that concentration of feeling which had eluded him in *Diane au bois* and no doubt he would have been among the first to give Verlaine credit for this.

In the latter half of 1887 Debussy set to work on two projects which capitalized on the ability he had shown in the Verlaine settings for capturing the voice of a poet: *La damoiselle élue* on the poem by Dante Gabriel Rossetti, and the *Cinq poèmes de Baudelaire*. Indeed whereas until now his settings of Gautier, Bourget, Leconte de Lisle or Banville had been barely distinguishable from one another, from here on he was to find quite individual 'substyles' for each poet (Verlaine, Baudelaire, Pierre Louÿs, Mallarmé, as well as for the trio of ancient poets: Charles d'Orléans, Tristan Lhermite and François Villon). At the same time, each of these substyles remains within what is recognizably a Debussyan style overall – an astonishing achievement for which the composer has perhaps not been given sufficient credit.

After the art critic Philippe Burty had visited London in 1869 for the Royal Academy exhibition, he reported in a Paris magazine that the Pre-Raphaelites, and especially Burne-Jones, practised 'the patient and humble observation which had been brought to painting by the Italian primitives'.[4] It is hardly surprising that this aspect of Pre-Raphaelitism should attract a young composer fresh from a productive contact with Botticelli. As Richard Langham Smith has pointed out, 'the 1880s mark the beginning of Debussy's published work and also the period when the vogue for Pre-Raphaelitism really took off in France'. But by 1884 no Rossetti painting had been exhibited in France and Debussy's contact with the artist came through reproductions and through translations of his poetry, including those by Gabriel Sarrazin whose prose version of The Blessed Damozel he used for his cantata. An article by Sarrazin on the painting of that name suggests a critic straining at the impossible: 'a subtle blue glow escaped from the Blessed Damozel's lowered eyelids and, from the height of the gilded battlements of heaven, descended, with the languors of a sublime love, upon the lover constrained in earthly exile'. Happily, Sarrazin's translation of the poem is less heavily weighed down with epithets so that Debussy was left some room to manoeuvre. But at least Sarrazin's article had for the first time 'clarified the view of the "ange-femme" as typifying Rossetti's exploration of the tension between the mystical and the fleshly'.

Debussy duly sent the completed cantata to the Institut towards the end of 1888 as the third of his four statutory envois. The Académie des Beaux-Arts responded in January 1889:

The chosen text is in prose and rather obscure. But the music he has set it to is devoid neither of poetry nor of charm, even though it still smacks of those modish, systematic tendencies in expression and form for which the Academy has already had occasion to upbraid the composer. In this work, at any rate, his inclinations and these procedures manifest themselves more discreetly and seem, up to a certain point, to be justified by the very nature and the indeterminate character of the subject.[5]

One could easily fill several pages with an 'explication' of this text! There is an implied criticism of Debussy for having chosen a text in prose rather than in verse, but the fact that he has made it poetic alleviates the crime – Debussy was to pursue this path further a decade later. Then, charm seems to represent a bonus point. Against this there are again the Impressionist tendencies deplored in *Printemps*, but these again are alleviated by discretion and relevance to the text. While a full deconstruction of the text might reveal that it was a blanket statement, trying desperately to convey the divergent viewpoints of the six members of the jury, it might reasonably be summarized as saying 'this music has got something but we're not quite sure what; all in all, the fence seems the most appropriate place for us'. Debussy might reasonably have taken some comfort from the verdict.

The atmosphere of *La damoiselle élue* is both refined and sensuous, matching the mystical yet fleshly angel-woman of the title. The scope of the musical language is now somewhat broader, with the church modes bringing both a whiff of incense and a resonance of things far away and long ago. To this is added one of the earliest intimations that Debussy's love of Wagner had moved on from distant worship to active involvement. In the summer of 1888 he joined one of the fashionable pilgrimages from Paris to hear *Parsifal* and *The Mastersingers* at Bayreuth, where other members of the party included Fauré and André Messager, who was later to conduct the first performances of *Pelléas*. Unfortunately no letters from Debussy survive to tell of this visit, but *La damoiselle*, for all that Debussy later boasted to his friend

Pierre Louÿs that he had succeeded in not imitating *Parsifal*, marks the entry point of that music drama into Debussy's innermost soul.

The very fact that he needed to make the boast indicates that escaping from Wagner demanded a conscious effort on his part. That he in fact failed to escape is no cause for censure, if only because, as Robin Holloway has pointed out, 'in *La damoiselle* Debussy has remembered moments from Wagner for which his individual sensibility feels a particular predilection. This "lexicon of Wagner's most intimate phrases" he incorporates into his own style and method, in every other respect quite different from Wagner.'[6] This ability to dissociate sounds from their traditional (or even not so traditional) function was to remain one of Debussy's most powerful tools in revolutionising musical grammar and syntax.

From a more personal angle, his welcoming of Wagner and Rossetti into his life underlines the urge to reinvent himself on his return from Rome. Marguerite Vasnier tells us that he had changed, and Debussy himself tells us that old comrades like Pierné, Vidal and Leroux no longer seemed interested in him. True, he was still living with his parents, but the indications are that he spent most of his time in haunts like Le chat noir or in cafés talking with writers like Villiers de l'Isle Adam, Catulle Mendès, Gabriel Mourey and Jean Moréas, as well as with journalists and painters. Throughout his life, he was to nurse a particular hatred of musicians talking music, and the two composers he got to know around this time were both men of wide culture and elitist tendencies.

Paul Dukas, a little younger than Debussy, had entered Guiraud's composition class in 1885 and was awarded a Second Prix de Rome in 1888. After failing to win the First Prize the following year, 'he left the Conservatoire and got seriously down to work', as one recent dictionary puts it. He was very much his own man, like Debussy, and was, if possible, even more self-critical: between 1912 and his death in 1935 he published only two short pieces, one of them in Debussy's memory. As François Lesure records,

On 25 May 1887, the day of the Opéra-Comique fire, Achille gave his friend a copy of the new edition of Mallarmé's L'après-midi d'un faune with the dedication: 'Friendship, aesthetic outlook . . . the whole gamut' (Amitiés, Esthétique . . . Toute la lyre). Both indulged their musical curiosity, playing Palestrina motets and masses as piano duets (!). Achille introduced him to the Balakirev and Borodin songs he had brought back from Russia, and commented on everything as he went through with a 'C'est bien!' in that particular tone of voice which with him indicated admiration.[7]

Ernest Chausson was seven years older than Debussy, who was later to refer to him as filling the role of an elder brother. After studying briefly with Massenet, Chausson joined the bande à Franck in the early 1880s and took advantage of his private means to refine and agonize over his works with an intensity that Debussy was occasionally to make gentle fun of. His symphonic poem Viviane of 1882 may well have been inspired by Burne-Jones's painting 'Merlin and Viviane' and throughout his rather brief friendship with Debussy he was working on a three-act opera Le roi Arthus.

Like Debussy, Chausson felt the need to find his own voice and not rely either on Wagner or, in his case, on César Franck. As Robin Holloway says, Debussy was clever enough or genius enough to take from Wagner just those isolated elements he found useful. Chausson, an indisputably lesser artist though a distinctly interesting one, seems to have had a harder time disengaging himself from the whole fervid, passionate, plangent atmosphere surrounding Franck and exuded by much of his music. The Chausson/Debussy correspondence is highly illuminating about them both and will be cited shortly. But a month before Debussy's first known letter to Chausson of 7 March 1889 the two men and Fauré shared a concert of the Société nationale, of which Debussy had been elected a member a year earlier and for which both Chausson and Fauré were active committee members.

This concert on 2 February appears to have been the first time Debussy's music was played in these august surroundings. The tenor Maurice Bagès sang two of the Ariettes, accompanied by the composer, while Fauré was represented by his Second Piano Quartet and Chausson by his incidental music to The Tempest. Given that the concert took place only four days after the Académie had published their not unfavourable report on La damoiselle, Debussy could be excused for being in a state of heightened awareness. This is borne out by the impact the Fauré and Chausson works had on him: the details of each will be considered in the discussion of the String Quartet (p. 75) and of Pelléas et Mélisande (pp. 103–4) respectively. As to the two (unidentified) songs from the Ariettes, the critic of the Guide musical told his readers on 7 February that Achille Debussy demonstrated a 'refined, delicate artistic nature that seeks out the new and eschews banality. Pretty piano textures in the accompaniment. At times a slight tendency towards the affected and precious. But would anyone ever think M. Debussy had been through the Conservatoire?' The composer must, I think, have been thrilled by that last remark: the art that concealed art was ever to be his goal.

A few weeks later he finished his Cinq poèmes de Baudelaire which had occupied him, on and off, for the last fifteen months. Debussy's Baudelaire substyle is quite different from his Verlaine one, and in determining it Debussy engineered a fruitful rapprochement between his response to the poems from Les fleurs du mal and Baudelaire's own musical tastes. When a concert of Wagner's works was given in Paris in 1860, Baudelaire had been swept off his feet; and when Tannhäuser was whistled off the Opéra stage a year later, he published a spirited defence of the man and his music. The concert of 1860 had established that 'as a writer for the orchestra, as an artist translating through the myriad combinations of sound the tumults of the human soul, Richard Wagner was working at the highest level and was indeed as great as the greatest'.[8] In the Fleurs du mal itself, he says that 'music often sweeps me away like a tide (La musique souvent me prend comme une mer)' and that 'I feel vibrating within me all the passions of a ship in labour.'[9]

The choice therefore of a Wagnerian substyle for the Cinq poèmes can be seen as a natural one, provided Debussy was able to tame Wagner in vibrating, passionate mode. Opinions may differ over his success in this. But it is plainly true that, as Holloway says, 'these wonderful songs are somewhat outside the mainstream of Debussy's development'. And this time Debussy has opted for *Tristan and Isolde* rather than *Parsifal*. In the first song, 'Le balcon', written in January 1888, before he had been to Bayreuth, the spiritual affinity is with 'the more reflective passages near the beginning of *Tristan* Act II as Isolde awaits her lover (for example, vocal score pp. 138–40; 145–9; 152–9). The exceptionally complicated piano part in the Debussy has very much the feel (and to a certain extent the sound) of an orchestral transcription; the texture it most closely resembles is of these pages in the piano-score of *Tristan*'.[10] We do well to remember that in those days before gramophone recordings the piano and piano duet were the favourite vehicles for learning orchestral scores. It is not surprising that Debussy, as a particularly adept score-reader and a composer highly sensitive to the feel of music on the keyboard (as his later piano pieces testify) should have adapted the slightly thick and awkward style typical of orchestral transcriptions to his own ends.

That the style of the *Cinq poèmes* was a conscious choice, and not evidence of a Debussy helplessly and irrevocably in thrall to the master of Bayreuth, can be seen from one of his most popular early works written around the same time – first performed indeed in March 1889, the very month in which he completed the *Cinq poèmes*.

The most usually heard version of the *Petite suite* is the orchestral arrangement by Henry Busser, published in 1907, but it was originally scored for piano duet. The performers in 1889 were the composer and his future publisher, Jacques Durand, who later recalled:

> In an attempt to do something to persuade music lovers of the charm of the *Petite suite*, it was agreed with Debussy that the two of us should give a performance of it at a Paris salon frequented by the élite among the dictators of fashion. The performance took place and the reception was kind, but no more than that; I was well aware that we had not broken through.
>
> Debussy was very nervous before sitting down at the piano with

me and had urged me not to go too fast. I promised. But hardly had we begun when Debussy began to hurry; and despite all my efforts, I was unable to hold him back. He was in haste to put this public trial behind him. So I followed the somewhat hectic tempi as best I could, and the work finished with a brio that was, probably, an important factor in the polite sympathy with which the work was finally greeted.

Durand is here being slightly unkind. If the Académie des Beaux-Arts were looking for charm, then it is to be found in this suite in abundance. The distance from Wagner and Baudelaire is vast (the 'Menuet' is actually a reworking of a Banville song, 'Fête galante', of 1882) and there are one or two of the slightly clumsy transitions which still plagued Debussy at this period, but the tunefulness and individuality of the melodies show what a successful, and rich, composer of light music he could have become, had he not been summoned to greater things.

Two events of 1889 give us a clue as to Debussy's thoughts and susceptibilities. The first was the Universal Exhibition, set up in the Champ de Mars and the surrounding areas and crowned by M. Eiffel's new tower. We may presume that Debussy as a fifteen-year-old had gone to the 1878 Exhibition and heard the music of the Hungarian gypsies and the Tunisian and Algerian café orchestras. But we have no evidence, although he was later greatly moved by a gypsy fiddler on his visit to Budapest. The 1889 Exhibition brought the Annamite theatre (from the central Eastern region of Vietnam, straddling the present North/South divide) and a group of four young female Javanese dancers. The influence of the Javanese gamelan on Debussy's music has been well charted over the years, and will be noted here when necessary. But that of the Annamite theatre remains to be explored in any depth. Debussy's most public reference to it came in a newspaper article of February 1913:

In the Annamite theatre they present a sort of operatic embryo, influenced by China, in which one can recognize the formula of the Ring, only there are more Gods and fewer pieces of scenery . . . A small, furious clarinet is in charge of emotion; a tam-tam is the organizer of terror . . . and that's all! No purpose-built theatre, no hidden orchestra. Nothing but an instinctive need for art which has found an ingenious way of satisfying itself; not a trace of bad taste! – And when you consider those people have never had the notion of borrowing their formulae from the school of Munich: what can they be thinking of?

If we put aside the dig against Wagner – more or less obligatory for Debussy by 1913 – we find once again his obsession with economy of means.

Whether the Annamite music had any specific, local influence on his own remains unclear. But the general thrust of his thinking about opera (and, as I have said, every young French composer was encouraged to think on this thing) comes across from a résumé by his fellow student Maurice Emmanuel of conversations Debussy had with Ernest Guiraud in this same year of 1889. These took place at a Paris restaurant on a dozen or so occasions, with Emmanuel silent and listening eagerly and Guiraud, no doubt, paying the bill.[11]

For our purposes, a brief scattering of Debussy's more provocative comments must suffice. His ideal librettist would be someone

who only implies things and who would allow me to graft my dream on to his, who would invent characters belonging to no particular time or place; who would not despotically impose on me actions to be depicted and would leave me free, here and there, to surpass him in matters of art and to fill out his work . . . In opera there is too much singing . . . Nothing must hold up the sweep of the drama: every musical development not called for by the words is an error . . . I dream of librettos which do not condemn me to perpetrate acts that are long and heavy, but which give me scenes that are mobile and varied, as to both place and character; in which the actors don't discuss things but are victims of life and destiny.

On a more general musical front he was even more outspoken:

You must drown the sense of key . . . There is no theory. You have merely to listen. Pleasure is the law . . . I don't write in the fugal style, because I know it.

... all of which explains well enough Debussy's capacity to upset and outrage the Establishment. In September of the previous year he had refused to write the overture customarily demanded from a returning Prix de Rome winner for the Académie's annual concert, claiming he was unable to compose anything worthy of the occasion. But in October 1889, at the time he was favouring Guiraud and Emmanuel with his opinions, he did begin his fourth and last *envoi*, a *Fantaisie* for piano and orchestra (there is a possibility that he had already begun it in April, but he wrote 'October 1889' as the starting date on the autograph).

In the event, he never sent this to the Institut nor was it ever performed in his lifetime, though it came very close. The Société nationale programmed it for 21 April 1890, to be conducted by d'Indy. But after the final rehearsal d'Indy realized the concert was going to be too long, even for those days, and suggested playing just the first movement. Debussy's reponse was surreptitiously to remove the orchestral parts from the stands. Those biographers who cherish the image of Debussy the renegade have tended to report that he did so in a huff and as an act of hostility to the Société or to d'Indy personally. Alas for them, the truth is more prosaic, if more interesting. Writing to d'Indy next day, Debussy expressed his view that

> playing just the first movement of the *Fantaisie* is not only dangerous but must inevitably give a false impression of the whole. On reflection, I would rather have a passable performance of all three movements than a fine performance of the first through your good offices.
>
> It was not a rush of blood to the head nor any kind of ill feeling that moved me to take such drastic action. I hope anyway that you will agree with my point of view. Please believe me when I say how sorry I am to have been so apparently remiss in fulfilling my obligations towards you. You still have my gratitude, at least, and my sincere friendship.

There is no reason to doubt the sincerity of this letter as to either facts or feelings. True, Debussy might have expected d'Indy, as a

Franck pupil, to have understood without being told that the *Fantaisie* is cyclic and therefore that its three movements are indivisible, more especially as it may have been based on d'Indy's own *Symphonie cévenole* for piano and orchestra of 1886. But Debussy was clearly being careful not to offend further than he had to. The supposed animosity between the two composers has in any case been greatly exaggerated, notably by the critic Emile Vuillermoz, and Debussy was to serve three spells on the Société's committee between 1893 and 1902.

At various times in his life Debussy was to consider re-orchestrating the *Fantaisie* and changing the orchestra's relationship with the piano ('without which one is faced with a slightly ridiculous contest between the two characters', as he said in a letter to Varèse in August 1909), but never got round to bringing the work into what he considered a performable state. Changes he made on the second proofs, whether in 1890, 1895 or 1909 (all three dates have their champions), already constitute what amounts to a re-orchestration of many passages, distinguishing more clearly between the textures of themes on first and subsequent hearings and producing more effective crescendos. But 'there are no excised or added measures, no drastic harmonic alterations, indeed, no major changes that would alter the work's form'.[12] Any idea therefore that Debussy was unhappy with sonata or cyclic structures in principle is obviously wide of the mark.

With the non-submission of the *Fantaisie* to the Académie des Beaux-Arts Debussy signalled that his student days were over and, realistically, that this particular institution was no longer in a position to dictate or hinder his career. But before leaving the subject of Debussy's four *envois*, it is as well to note that, after the lost score of *Zuléima*, the subsequent trio of offerings (*Printemps*, *La damoiselle élue* and the *Fantaisie*) are all still in the mainstream repertory. Debussy's nearest rivals for success in this respect, Berlioz (with the *Resurrexit* that found a place in the *Requiem* and the *Rob Roy* overture) and Bizet (with *Don Procopio*, the ode-symphony *Vasco de Gama* and the scherzo of the *Roma* symphony), are some way off the pace.

This might seem to have been a natural point for Debussy to have launched out unequivocally on the 'musique à moi' he was always dreaming of. Instead, 1890 appears to have been a year of marking time with a number of charming but relatively conventional piano pieces, and even of retrogression with his attempts on a grand opera libretto by the poet and critic Catulle Mendès. Mendès was a passionate Wagnerian and in his text for *Rodrigue et Chimène* aimed at precisely the kinds of operatic effect against which Debussy had already inveighed in his conversations with Guiraud and elsewhere. To take but one example, in Act I scene 3 the men of Gormaz interrupt the two lovers, shouting

> Wine! Wine! Empty the cellars! Bring wine from Burgos and Irun!
> By St James, brave men don't hear Mass on an empty stomach!

Not entirely surprisingly, this libretto had been lying in Mendès's bottom drawer for twelve years and Debussy's only excuse for reviving it, and for managing to compose music for most of the first three of its four acts, can have been that he was even shorter of money than usual and that he needed something of the kind to try and force the doors of the Opéra. It was around the autumn of 1890 that Debussy was introduced to the poet Mallarmé, who had been impressed by the recently published *Cinq poèmes de Baudelaire* and who now asked him whether he would collaborate in a theatrical production of *L'après-midi d'un faune*. To have made the short walk from his rude labours on *Rodrigue* in his parents' apartment on the rue de Berlin (now rue de Liège) to Mallarmé's elitist Tuesday salon on the rue de Rome must have been a curious experience; but it may have been rather the journeys back again that finally made Debussy see the error of his ways after some three years of struggle.[13]

Together with the publication of the *Cinq poèmes de Baudelaire*, the other positive event of 1890 was Debussy's meeting with the twenty-four-year-old Gaby Dupont. François Lesure describes her as 'having an excellent figure, light brown hair which she dyed, a firm chin, blue-green eyes and a brilliant complexion'. Perhaps the desire to set up house with her prompted Debussy to pursue the hopefully profitable

Rodrigue? For the moment, though, he stayed in the rue de Berlin and limited his changes to one of name, from Achille to the Claude-Achille that appears on his baptismal certificate.

The Cinq poèmes were published in an edition of 150 copies by Edmond Bailly whose 'Librairie de l'art indépendant' in the rue de la Chaussée d'Antin was patronised by writers such as Henri de Régnier, André Gide and Ferdinand Hérold. Chausson too was a customer while Debussy, according to Victor-Emile Michelet, 'would come almost every day at the end of the afternoon . . . either on his own or with his good friend Erik Satie . . .'[14]

As a regular visitor to Mallarmé's Tuesdays and to Bailly's bookshop, Debussy found himself deep in what would nowadays be called 'alternative cultures'. It would certainly have been no hardship to him to find that Mallarmé and his Symbolist colleagues held music in very high esteem and that he, Debussy, was one of only three representatives of that art among the group, together with the ultra-respectable Chausson and d'Indy. The following two quotations from Mallarmé's prose writings are among many that chime in harmoniously with what we know of Debussy's aesthetics: 'things exist, we do not have to create them; we have only to grasp their relationships; and it is the threads of these relationships that make up poems and orchestras'; and 'everything sacred which wishes to remain sacred shrouds itself in mystery'.[15]

'Mystery' was also a key word for the considerable number of Bailly's customers who took an interest in the esoteric. Bailly himself in 1893 published several numbers of a review called La haute science, 'a documentary review of the esoteric tradition and of religious symbolism'. Whatever the depth of Debussy's interest in occult and Theosophical practices, or in the astrological input from the splendidly named Ely Star, he cannot but have been struck by Bailly's view of music which, quite probably as a result of conversations with Mallarmé, was in striking accord with the passage quoted above:

> I do not believe that the artist is a creator, in the proper sense of the word. It is easier for me to admit the existence of some immense

reservoir in which, from all time and for ever, is stored the ideal material of all imaginable manifestations of thought, and on which, by a deliberate phenomenon that puts into exceptional action certain mysterious workings of consciousness, it is allowed to draw, sometimes to perfection, in proportion to the quantity of the esthetic sense of him who perceives it.[16]

Did Debussy then come to be persuaded that there was in fact no such thing as a 'musique à moi'? If so, then his struggle was to tune his antennae to the music already existing in the 'immense reservoir' or in Nature (supposing those two to be distinct entities); as he put it more poetically in his article on 'Taste' in February 1913:

When the god Pan fitted together the seven reeds of his pipe, he began merely by imitating the long, melancholy note of the toad complaining to the rays of the moon. Later, he struggled with the song of the birds. It was probably from that moment that the birds began to enrich their repertoire.

Such origins are quite sacred enough for music to take some pride in them and preserve an element of mystery . . . In the name of all the gods, let us not try to do away with it any more than to explain it.

Debussy may well have spent many an hour tuning in to the infinite, but he still had to live. His two groups of composition completed in 1891 partake of both the infinite and the finite. As to the latter, he was commissioned by a General Meredith Read to make a setting of the March of the ancient Counts of Ross from whom the general was descended. A picturesque legend has grown up whereby the two men, unable to understand each other's language, had to repair to a café and employ Alphonse Allais as an interpreter. Sadly, this entertaining cameo has to be false. John Meredith Read (1837–96) was an 'American lawyer, diplomat, and writer, who during the Civil War had acted as adjutant-general of New York. During 1868–73 he was US consul-general for France, and 1873–79 resident minister for Greece'.[17] It is inconceivable that such a man of parts, with five years diplomatic service in France, would have needed an interpreter for such a simple request; though no doubt the contract may have been sealed by a drink at one of the composer's favourite haunts, such as the taverne Pousset or the café Vachette.

Debussy approached more nearly to the infinite in 1891 in three settings of poems by Verlaine, whom he had now met at Mallarmé's *mardis* – although, unfortunately, there is no record of Verlaine hearing or commenting on the *Ariettes*, the only Debussy settings of his poetry published in his lifetime.

The poems for the *Trois mélodies* come from Verlaine's collection *Sagesse*. In the first song, 'La mer est plus belle que les cathédrales', Debussy of course picks up on the sweep of the sea but combines this with a number of 'religious', that is modal, inflections to produce an extraordinarily rich picture of the sea as 'more beautiful than all, better than us'. Keen ears will also detect an early appearance of the 'Mélisande motif' at the words 'Oh! si patiente, même quand méchante' (Oh! so patient, even when savage) . . . In the third song, 'L'échelonnement des haies' (The line of the hedgerows), Debussy at times follows his own advice to 'drown the sense of key' – for instance on the lines 'L'onde roulée en volutes, / De cloches comme des flûtes' (The wave furled in scrolls, / Bells like flutes), where the curling gestures of the piano take precedence over everything else.

But of the three, it is the second song, 'Le son du cor s'afflige vers les bois' (The sound of the horn goes grieving towards the woods), that gives the clearest sense of the direction Debussy's song writing was taking. The bare opening, with irregular rhythms gently jostling each other, leads to a voice entry on nine repeated notes, finally rising a semitone to the word 'bois': this is an utterly different world from the broad, Wagnerian paragraphs of the *Cinq poèmes* – a world dominated by throbbing chords, slowly changing harmonies and a single, brief, four-note figure in the piano part. The sense of key is well and truly drowned, too: we have to wait for the final chord of F major to tell us, by implication, that the previous thirty-eight bars were really in F minor.

From these three poems taken from *Sagesse* Debussy returned to another three from Verlaine's collection *Fêtes galantes* which he had already set ten years before. The bones of the sprightly 'Fantoches' remain much the same, with allowance made for the fact that Marie Vasnier's high notes no longer had to be catered for, but for 'Clair de lune' he made an entirely new setting. Fauré's version of the same poem had been published in 1888 and performed at a Société nationale concert the same year, so perhaps Debussy felt he was on his mettle. But the most interesting song in many ways is the opening 'En sourdine'. No fewer than five autographs exist of the 1882 version, suggesting that the poem had, like Banville's *Diane aux bois*, stirred resonances in him which he could not quite capture on paper. The 1892 version is, again, quite different in the musical figures it employs, but it goes still further than 'Le son du cor' in drowning the sense of key, even refusing to end on a simple common chord. As the American scholar Marie Rolf says,

> The concept of subtle understatement – so much a part of the Symbolist esthetic – is exercised in the later setting [of 'En sourdine'] in Debussy's use of a consistently low tessitura for the voice and in his frequent employment of a single pitch to deliver entire lines of text, such as on the words 'Calmes dans le demi-jour' or 'Laissons-nous persuader'. . . . Nor do we discover as many interior passages that are treated as musical sequences; rather, the later version utilizes a technique of continual spinning out or subtle variation of the melodic line, a device that becomes a permanent component of Debussy's mature compositional style.[18]

Two further points arise out of Dr Rolf's comments. First, the use of a fairly low tessitura and of repeated notes means that the words are given a prominence denied them in the higher flights of fancy inspired by Marie Vasnier: singing here reclaims its ancient French virtue of being merely heightened speech. Secondly, the absence of regular sequences (that is, straight repetitions of a passage at another, usually higher pitch) keeps the listener on the alert, willing to be guided not only by the music but by the poem. Obviously this technique only works if you choose a poet whose words are worth following.

One autograph of what was to be the first of two sets of *Fêtes galantes* on poems by Verlaine bears the date 'May 1892'. This was to be one of the crucial years in the composer's development, the one in which he took several large strides in that re-invention of himself he had begun on his return from Rome in 1887. For a start, he left his parents' home to share a furnished apartment at 42 rue de Londres with Gaby Dupont and, perhaps as a further sign of his new-found independence, dropped the 'Achille' from his name to become simply and finally 'Claude'. On 30 January he wrote to his friend Robert Godet on the subject of *Rodrigue et Chimène*:

> My life is hardship and misery thanks to this opera. Everything about it is wrong for me. I remember you used to like the colour of my pens – well, the poor things are sad and exhausted now. I long to see you and play you the two acts I've finished, because I'm afraid I may have won victories over my true self.

Whether or not he had that opportunity, before long his true self reasserted its rights and *Rodrigue* was definitively abandoned at some point before the end of 1893. Its irrelevance to his career was underlined by the three new works he now embarked on, and no less by a further experience of the music of the Renaissance polyphonists which had so impressed him in Rome. His friend and patron André Poniatowski remembered that the first time Mallarmé came to his house

> was on a Sunday morning, after a mass at Saint-Gervais where Debussy had taken us to hear Gregorian chant. Very soon these Sunday morning sessions at Saint-Gervais became extremely popular. Indeed, the numbers of our group grew to such an extent that the parishioners complained to their curé, because their seats were taken every Sunday by crowds of people who, it had to be said, listened to the sacred chants in exemplary silence, but usually with their backs to the main altar.

Maybe the chants were the only music Poniatowski remembered over fifty years later, but the services certainly included polyphony as well. The Holy Week services for 1892 in the church of Saint-Gervais, in central Paris just next to the Hôtel de Ville, included music by

Palestrina, Lassus, Victoria and Josquin, for which the conductor Charles Bordes had taken 103 rehearsals and d'Indy 50.[19] We may presume, I think, that the results of such careful and laborious preparation would have been heard beyond the confines of Holy Week itself.

Poniatowski goes on to say that he had tried to place the *Fantaisie* with American orchestras:

> My idea was that, if this work was successfully performed in New York, I might persuade someone like [Andrew] Carnegie to take an interest in Debussy's career and to offer him over a period of two or three years the material and spiritual tranquillity which he lacked entirely in Paris. None of his works had reached the general public and the piano lessons at five francs an hour, which provided his bread and butter, exasperated him – even before I left Paris he was heading for a nervous collapse . . .

Nothing came of the idea, partly, it seems, because a letter of Debussy's had gone astray. When Debussy's next letter of 5 October did reach Poniatowski, it certainly must have given that kind friend some reason to worry over the composer's emotional state:

> Whatever happens, I shall always be grateful to you for keeping me in mind, an act of imagination in an otherwise utilitarian world, and for helping me escape from the black hole which my life has tended to become. I shall have the courage now to keep going in spite of everything, the failures that crush even the strongest and the enemies ranged against me. It's strange, but even though my name is almost unknown there are innumerable people who detest me. They spread stories about me in Establishment circles, the sort of stories likely to give my music a bad smell for evermore. So you can understand easily enough how much I look forward to being rid of them, once and for all, and to satisfying my great ambition – to run my own show in my own way (*faire du théâtre à moi tout seul*) and root out the imbecility in musical understanding that these last few years have fostered in the gentle listeners of our time.

At the same time, it does not do to exaggerate Debussy's mental problems. As he says, Poniatowski's help provided him with 'the courage to keep going' and he did at least have an ambition to fulfil beyond the routine of giving piano lessons. Interestingly, his hopes for a 'musique à moi' had now grown somewhat to embrace a 'théâtre à moi'; perhaps Wagner's literal theatre was in the back of his mind, but it seems more reasonable to interpret 'théâtre' here not just as music *per se* but as everything music could bring with it in the way of being an educative, spiritual and moral force. One of the threads that runs through Debussy's writings about music is that so few people understand what it essentially is. And if we regard his attitude as conceited, so be it – as things transpired, he had a lot to be conceited about.

The three works he began in 1892 all follow this high road, taking their inspiration from the Symbolist milieu which he was finding congenial both for what it was (a hothouse of fruitful artistic ideas, emphasizing quality) and for what it was not (a factory of materialistic products, emphasizing quantity). Little, unfortunately, is known about one of the three works, the *Trois scènes au crépuscule* (Three Twilight Scenes) for orchestra. A couple of pages of sketches survive but nothing in these suggests that these scenes were the ancestors of the *Nocturnes*, as claimed by Léon Vallas. As for Debussy's claim to Poniatowski that they were 'almost finished' in September 1892, we can probably file it with other such claims under the heading 'fantaisies'; likewise his statement five months later that he had 'revised the *Scènes au crépuscule* quite extensively'. All we can be certain of is that they were inspired by a series of ten poems with that title by his friend Henri de Régnier, published in 1890 in his *Poèmes anciens et romanesques*.

Debussy's Symbolist leanings were expressed more fully and successfully in his set of four *Proses lyriques* for which he himself wrote the poems. Knights in search of the Holy Grail and Art Nouveau flower maidens blend with bells and songs of innocence: in the last song, 'De soir', 'a theme in the piano part is a popular tune to which all little French girls make a singing game, one of them representing the tower, while the others turn around her'.[20] Even though Debussy never went to school, he must have seen little girls playing this game and remembered the tune. The value and power of distant memories was a favourite theme of the Symbolists, as it was to be of Marcel Proust, and certainly there is no dissonance in Debussy's song between this remembered popular tune and the more obviously 'artistic' lines and harmonies that surround it. The whole cycle made a tremendous impression on the twenty-year-old Ravel when it was published in 1895, not least through the *ennui* breathed by the third song, 'De fleurs', in which lines such as 'Come, come, redeeming hands! / Break the panes of falsehood, / Break the panes of evildoing, / My soul is dying of too much sun!' appealed to the general perception of adolescents that the world was a hard, unsympathetic place. It may not be wholly frivolous to note too that in a questionnaire of 1889 Debussy, as well as choosing Hamlet as his favourite fictional hero, Gustave Moreau as one of his favourite painters and his favourite occupation as 'reading while smoking complicated blends of tobacco', had identified his idea of misery as 'being too hot'![21]

While the music of these songs does not return to the luxuriant textures of the *Poèmes de Baudelaire*, there is nonetheless a feeling at times that Debussy is working a shade too hard to accommodate all the riches of his free-verse text. This problem of the simultaneous pacing of words and music was easier to solve when, as with Verlaine, so much was implicit in the verse rather than explicit. Another solution altogether was to absorb the message, the atmosphere of a poem, and then recreate them in purely instrumental terms. How Debussy brought this technique to bear on Mallarmé's *L'après-midi d'un faune* I shall discuss in the next chapter. For the moment, suffice it to say that, given the difficulty of the task, two years spent writing some nine minutes of music was not an inordinately long time.

The year 1893 continued to witness the composer's spiritual if not material progress. On 8 April the Société nationale programmed *La damoiselle élue* – the first performance of any of his orchestral works. The concert also included an overture by Dukas, Chausson's *Poème de l'amour et de la mer* and the first performance of the orchestral version of Duparc's song *Phidylé*. The critic of *Le figaro*, Charles Darcours,

Your favourite virtue.	L'orgueil
Your favourite qualities in man.	La Volonté
Your favourite qualities in woman.	Le charme.
Your favourite occupation.	Lire en fumant des tabacs compliqués.
Your chief characteristic.	mes cheveux.
Your idea of happiness.	Aimer.
Your idea of misery.	Avoir trop chaud.
Your favourite colour and flower.	Violet.
If not yourself, who would you be?	Marin.
Where would you like to live?	n'importe où. hors du monde.
Your favourite prose authors.	Flaubert. Edgard. Poë
Your favourite poets.	Baudelaire.
Your favourite painters and composers.	Botticelli. Gustave Moreau. Palestrina. Bach. Wagner.
Your favourite heroes in real life.	Skobeleff.
Your favourite heroines in real life.	Madame de Beaumont.
Your favourite heroes in fiction.	Hamlet
Your favourite heroines in fiction.	Rosalinde
Your favourite food and drink.	La cuisine russe. Le café.
Your favourite names.	Cela dépend des gens
Your pet aversion.	Les dilettantes, les femmes trop jolies
What characters in history do you most dislike.	Hérode.
What is your present state of mind?	Triste et chercheur. excité le 16 fév 89
For what fault have you most toleration?	Les fautes d'harmonie.
Your favourite motto.	Toujours plus haut.

3   Debussy's answers to a questionnaire put to him by a young girl in 1889

who had been generous in his praise of Debussy's cantatas in 1883
and 1884, now seized the opportunity to set *La damoiselle* up against
the other works in the concert. The score 'is not a masterpiece', he
wrote,

4   Gustave Moreau: *The Voices*

but on its own it contains more life than all the works that preceded it on the programme [it was placed last]. *La damoiselle élue* is a work that is at least original, extremely striking and very modern. Since your critic a few days ago was so warmly admiring the supreme beauties of Palestrina, he felt an almost culpable attraction when listening to the work, because it is a deeply sensual composition, decadent, even a touch rotten, but containing passages of shimmering charm. And it's so good to have a little youthful freshness! We are told that M. Debussy joined the Société nationale only by accident. Here, even so, is the new blood that venerable institution needs. This subcutaneous injection may well produce dangerous eruptions in the young composers of the future; but the society should be aware that an accident is less serious than death![22]

Debussy's friends Dukas and Chausson seem to have weathered with good humour the implication that they were over the hill. More interesting perhaps is Darcours' implied comparison of *La damoiselle* with the music of Palestrina. It is almost as though he felt Debussy was entering the Palestrinian soundworld, but then giving it a delightfully naughty twist that made of it something 'very modern'. He was certainly right about the 'dangerous eruptions' Debussy was to bring about in the younger generation.

Not that *La damoiselle* would ever be the chief culprit. That glory was to belong to a work whose inception can be dated very precisely to a theatrical performance at the Théâtre des Bouffes-Parisiens on Wednesday, 17 May 1893 – of Maurice Maeterlinck's play *Pelléas et Mélisande*. (Although we have no evidence, it is tempting to think that Satie might have joined him in the stalls on this his twenty-seventh birthday.) Debussy later intimated that he had already read the play, which was published the previous year, but clearly it was experiencing the drama in the theatre that touched off the desire to turn it into an opera. Henry Fouquier, reviewing the performance next day in *Le figaro*, responded to the generally low level of the lighting by saying that 'the more obscure something is, the happier are the real Symbolists, who get irritated when people start understanding things'. A connection suggests itself between the danger of too much sun, darkness in things physical, obscurity in things mental, and a loosening, even a 'rottenness' in the stays that held traditional musical syntax together . . .

Maeterlinck gave permission in August for Debussy to set his play

5   Ernest Chausson, Raymond Bonheur, Debussy and Mme Chausson on the
     banks of the Marne, 1893

and to make whatever cuts he thought necessary. In the meantime
Debussy played one of two pianos in an illustrated lecture on *Das
Rheingold* and *Die Walküre*, given by his librettist for *Rodrigue*, Catulle
Mendès, and attended the premiere of *Die Walküre* (or rather *La
Walkyrie*) at the Opéra in May. Then, at the end of the month,
Chausson had the happy idea of inviting Debussy to make two short
visits to the country house he and his family were renting at Luzancy
on the banks of the Marne, and for the next ten months or so their
friendship was marked by what François Lesure has called 'almost
excessive epistolary demonstrations'.

The reason seems to have been simply that each needed the other.
Debussy refers to Chausson's 'intervention in my life' as one of his
greatest pieces of good fortune, the word 'intervention' indicating, I
think, that on whatever front, moral, spiritual, social or financial,
Chausson had, like Poniatowski before him, dragged his young friend

out of some black hole. Chausson's need was more purely musical. While revering the memory of César Franck, who had died at the end of 1890, he recognized the necessity of freeing his music, rhythmically and texturally, from its Franckian tendencies towards an over-insistent solidity. He thus found himself in the paradoxical situation of asking the advice of Debussy-as-free-spirit while simultaneously urging him to toe the bourgeois social line (and, presumably, either marry Gaby or leave her).

Excessive or not, their epistolary demonstrations are highly illuminating. Four brief extracts from Debussy's side of the correspondence, from August to October, must suffice:

> My gratitude to you is greater than I can say and I'm profoundly happy to be your friend, because in you artistic qualities are complemented by human ones and, when you're kind enough to show me your music, you can't imagine the great sympathy I feel for you, seeing you at work with emotions which to me are foreign, but whose expression by you fills me with joy.

> The bell has now tolled to mark my thirty-first year, and I'm still not confident that my musical attitudes are right; and there are things I can't yet do (write masterpieces, for example, or, among other things, be completely serious – I'm too prone to dream my life away and to see realities only at the very moment they become insuperable).

> Music really ought to have been a hermetical science, enshrined in texts so hard and laborious to decipher as to discourage the herd of people who treat it as casually as they do a handkerchief! I'd go further and, instead of spreading music among the populace, I propose the foundation of a 'Society of Musical Esotericism' . . .

> One thing I'd like to see you free yourself from is your preoccupation with the inner parts of the texture. By which I mean that too often we're concerned with the frame before we've got the picture; it was our friend Richard Wagner, I think, who got us into this fix . . . It would be more profitable, I feel, to go about things the other way round, that's to say, to find the perfect expression for an idea and

add only as much decoration as is absolutely necessary . . . Look at Bach, where everything conspires wonderfully to highlight the central idea and where the delicacy of the inner parts never absorbs the principal line.

Debussy's dissatisfaction with his own work was chronic, but entirely explicable when his aims are analysed in terms of these apparently contradictory elements of simplicity and elitism. Any performer of his music soon discovers this contradiction to lie at its heart: that the fewer the notes, the harder it is to elicit their deepest meaning (see, for example, 'Des pas sur la neige' or 'The Little Shepherd').

The autumn of 1893 was spent on the first sketches for *Pelléas et Mélisande*, and on later and final drafts of *L'après-midi* (a version of which he played to de Régnier around the end of August) and of his String Quartet. He had 'finished' this in February, but continued to rethink the last movement at least until July. The Ysaÿe Quartet gave the first performance at the Société nationale on 29 December and for the most part the critics responded with a cautious silence. Of those who did respond, Guy Ropartz, an ex-pupil of Franck, noted a Russian influence and some unusual sonorities, while Willy, Colette's husband and an influential chronicler of the Paris music scene, confessed he found the work 'baffling', yet 'full of originality and charm' – a judgement remarkably similar to the one passed nearly five years earlier by the Académie des Beaux-Arts on *La damoiselle élue* (see p. 52).

The Society was not in an enormous hurry to repeat the Quartet – it was next programmed on 20 April 1895 – but at least Debussy had now met the Establishment on its own ground without disgrace. It is not without interest that in so doing he had fostered memories of his music's first appearance at the Société nationale on 2 February 1889. That concert had included Fauré's Second Piano Quartet. The opening bars of Debussy's Quartet clearly look back to those of Fauré's; at the same time, a comparison of the two passages shows to what utterly distinct worlds they belong for all their common ground in a modal G minor, and how even such a seasoned and intelligent critic as Willy might have been bemused by Debussy's instant plunging of the listener into uncharted waters. Three weeks earlier the anarchist Auguste Vaillant had thrown a bomb full of metal nails from the public gallery of the French parliament. Debussy's Quartet, if physically less threatening, nonetheless confirmed that the string quartet medium was unlikely ever to be the same again.

4 Scandals and masterpieces (1894–1901)

It had been Debussy's intention to dedicate his String Quartet to Chausson. But Chausson seems to have disapproved of the work, or at least of some aspects of it. This has to be deduced from Debussy's side of their correspondence, in which he moves quite smartly from defending his own position to attacking Chausson's. On 5 February 1894 he wrote:

> I should also say that I was really upset for several days by what you said about my quartet, as I felt that after all it only increased your partiality for *certain things* which I would rather it had encouraged you to forget. Anyway I'll write another one which will be for you, in all seriousness for you, and I'll try and bring some nobility to my forms. I'd like to have enough influence with you to be able to grumble at you and tell you you're heading in the wrong direction! ... You don't let yourself go enough and in particular you don't seem to allow enough play to that mysterious force which guides us towards the true expression of a feeling, whereas dedicated, single-minded searching only weakens it ... One has to tell oneself that when it comes to art we are nothing, merely the instrument of some destiny, and we have to allow it to fulfil itself!

... at which point we rejoin Mallarmé and Edmond Bailly and the 'reservoir of ideas'.

Debussy never did write a second String Quartet and, if he even contemplated one whose ennobled forms would please his friend, events on the social front soon put any such thoughts out of his mind. Early in 1894, possibly as a result of the performance of the String Quartet, Debussy found himself invited to the prestigious Friday salon of Mme de Saint-Marceaux. Rather different perspectives on the meeting come from the two sides in the encounter:

> Mme de Saint-Marceaux: In the evening, dinner in my apartment and music with Debussy. He made me sing La demoiselle élue [sic]. It's impossible to explain better than he does what he intends or intended. His voice is bad, but one gets used to it because the expression in it is so true (tant l'accent en est juste).[1]

> Debussy: Then there's Mme de Saint-Marceaux who's discovered that I'm a first-rate talent! It's enough to make you die laughing. But really, you'd have to be a hopelessly weak character to be taken in by all this rubbish.

And did he therefore find other things to do on his Friday evenings from there on? He did not. On Friday 9 March Mme de Marceaux noted: 'Debussy played L'après-midi d'un faune. One needs the orchestra in order to judge properly. But even so, the music is interesting.'[2]

In the meantime, on 17 February, the last two of the Proses lyriques were heard at a Société nationale concert in the Salle Pleyel with the composer accompanying a soprano called Thérèse Roger. The next thing any of his friends knew was that the two of them were engaged. On 1 March she sang in what the composer referred to as 'the Debussy festival' in Brussels, the first ever all-Debussy concert, including the same two songs from Proses lyriques, La damoiselle élue (at d'Indy's instigation) and the String Quartet. A week later Debussy opened his heart to Chausson:

> Now that a sunny road is open before me I'm afraid at not having deserved such happiness, and at the same time I'm fiercely determined to defend it with all the power at my disposal! Your advice about marriage has touched me deeply, I assure you, and it seems to me (novice that I am in the business) absolutely right . . . I really feel

6   Thérèse Roger

I've offered my life once and for all and that from now on it will be lived for just one person!

Unfortunately, anyone visiting 42 rue de Londres would quite reasonably have come to the conclusion that that one person was Gaby Dupont. Needless to say, this situation could not stay unresolved for long. Rumours began to circulate and on 17 March Mme de Saint-Marceaux confided to her diary that the marriage had been called off. Five days later, Debussy's friend Pierre Louÿs sent her a firm letter defending the composer's conduct, but to no avail. Her diary entry for 6 April reads: 'The break-up of Debussy's marriage is the central topic of our little group. Friends try and justify him. But unfortunately the truth is impossible to establish.'

The *bien pensants* denizens of that salon and others did not, it seems,

7   Gaby Dupont, August 1893

feel like giving Debussy the benefit of the doubt. Even the innocent
Mlle Roger did not dare show her face at Mme de Saint-Marceaux's for
another four years. As for poor Chausson, to some extent the architect
of the marriage and a proponent of Debussy's bourgeoisification, his
embarrassment was practically terminal. Relations with the culprit

8   Pierre Louÿs at his harmonium

ceased abruptly and on 6 April he wrote to his brother-in-law, the painter Henri Lerolle:

> Naturally Mme Roger [Thérèse's mother] spoke to me about Debussy, and in considerable detail ... I can see how he might have told lies, watered down the truth or put a different slant on things, even though that's a stupid and pointless way of behaving, but to lie directly to her face, with indignant protests, about something so serious, that I cannot comprehend.

Chausson's place as brother confessor was taken by the twenty-four-year-old writer Pierre Louÿs (pronounced 'Louee') who had stood up so stoutly for Debussy during the *affaire*. The two had met the previous year and numbered André Gide and Paul Valéry among their mutual acquaintances. Both these writers valued Louÿs highly as a friend and as a writer and certainly his was no ordinary spirit, as we can judge from information supplied by Edward Lockspeiser:

> In 1891, at the age of 21, Louÿs had inherited 300,000 francs. In March of that year he was afflicted with tuberculosis and was warned

that he might have only three years to live unless he led an abstemious existence. He determined, however, to spend 100,000 francs each year, bringing himself to ruin on Christmas Eve 1894. Until the success of his novel *Aphrodite* two years later Louÿs was supported by his brother.[3]

We should not be misled by the fact that in March 1894 Louÿs was still engaged in ridding himself of his considerable fortune into thinking that he was useful to Debussy only as a source of funds. Even if Louÿs was not a professional musician like Chausson, he was extremely responsive to music and was even something of a keyboard player: in a letter of 20 July 1894, Debussy lamented his absence because 'nobody else plays me Bach with those delightfully imaginative touches with which you alone know how to adorn such antiquities'. Of course, what Debussy calls Louÿs's 'délicieuse fantaisie' may indicate that the playing was neither orthodox nor perhaps wholly accurate. But obviously it was the spirit of his friend's performances that mattered.

For us, Louÿs is especially valuable as the recipient of letters written while Debussy was simultaneously engaged on three masterpieces between the summers of 1894 and 1895: *Prélude à l'après-midi d'un faune*, *Pelléas et Mélisande* and the earliest sketches for the three orchestral *Nocturnes*. After nearly a year's work on *Pelléas*, Debussy informed Louÿs in the July letter quoted above that he was about to tackle the vault scene (Act III scene 2) 'in a manner which you'll be good enough to find interesting when you see it'.

A month later, Debussy had written that scene and one more, and was busy on a third – for once, he may have been telling the truth when he said his life was as simple as a blade of grass and that he had no pleasures apart from working. By September he had also finished *L'après-midi* and on 20 December he invited Mallarmé to come to the first performance at a Société nationale concert next day:

Cher maître, I need not say how happy I should be if you were kind enough to honour with your presence the arabesque which, by an excess of pride perhaps, I believe to have been dictated by the flute of your faun.

Mallarmé had already heard Debussy play the work on the piano in the apartment Debussy had now moved to on the rue Gustave-Doré and, according to the composer's testimony in a letter of March 1910, had, while expressing surprise, commented that 'this music prolongs the emotion of my poem and conjures up the scenery more vividly than any colour'. He duly attended the performance on 22 December, contributing to what the conductor, Gustave Doret, described as

> a vast silence in the hall as I ascended the podium and our splendid flautist, Barrère, unfolded his opening line. All at once I felt behind me, as some conductors can, an audience that was totally spell-bound. It was a complete triumph, and I had no hesitation in breaking the rule forbidding encores.

Mallarmé was, it seems, for all his elitist tendencies, pleased with the work and its success in the eyes of the public. The critics, needless to say, resented the way in which an encore had attempted to render them redundant and scattered their fire wildly – from 'a lack of passion or vigour' to 'the preponderant influence of Wagner takes away from the composer the style he might command'!

A detailed analysis of *L'après-midi* or of its importance for twentieth-century music lies beyond the scope of the present biography. But as usual, the composer's own description of the piece, in a letter to Willy of 10 October 1895, is very much to the point:

> The *Prélude à l'après-midi d'un faune*, cher Monsieur, is it perhaps the dream left over at the bottom of the faun's flute? To be more precise, it is the general impression of the poem. If the music were to follow it more closely, it would run out of breath, like a dray-horse competing for the Grand Prix with a thoroughbred. It also demonstrates a disdain for the 'constructional knowhow' (*science de castors*) which is a burden upon our finest intellects . . . All the same, it follows the ascending shape of the poem as well as the scenery so marvellously

described in the text . . . As for the ending, it's a prolongation of the last line:

Couple farewell, I go to see what you became.

Taking their cue from this last remark, various critics have reasonably suggested that the opening flute phrase too refers to one particular line of the poem: 'une sonore, vaine et monotone ligne' – 'sonore' because the first note, C♯, was naturally out of tune on French flutes of the period and rectifying this produced a peculiarly veiled tonal quality; 'monotone' because the phrase is immediately repeated; and, perhaps most interestingly, 'vaine' or 'ineffectual' because the line generates none of the urgent forward thrust typical of 'first subjects' in a German symphony. Here for the first time Debussy was able to raise his 'plaisir' to the heights of a constructive principle.

The year 1895 was given over in part to various projected collaborations with Louÿs and even, momentarily, to a revision of the *Fantaisie* which the conductor Edouard Colonne was planning to put on at one of his concerts in the autumn. But nothing came of any of these plans. In the meantime, his life continued to be as simple as a blade of grass as he worked on his opera, finishing the first version in August. He wrote to Henri Lerolle on the 17th of that month:

> I think you'll like the scene in front of the cave. I tried to capture all the mystery of the night and the silence in which a blade of grass roused from its slumber makes an alarming noise . . .

And of Mélisande's death scene:

> Whenever a woman dies in the French theatre, it has to be like the *Lady of the Camellias*; though you're allowed to replace the camellias with some other flowers and the Lady with an Eastern princess! People can't get used to the idea that one might take one's leave discreetly like somebody who has had enough of planet Earth and is on their way to where the flowers of tranquillity bloom!

With the completion of the vocal score of *Pelléas*, Debussy's fears began to grow of what a realization of the opera might actually be like.

As his letters tell us, he had no high opinion of the musical Establishment of his time, any more than he had in general of salon hostesses. It cannot be said, therefore, that he threw himself heart and soul into the task of finding a conductor or a director or a theatre. Instead, *Pelléas* lived an underground existence for the next six and a half years while Debussy, at first no doubt mentally exhausted by his labours, waited in fearful hope for some angel to appear and take charge.

The only major event in his life in 1896 was the wild success of Louÿs's erotic novel *Aphrodite*, which appeared first in instalments in the magazine *Mercure de France* and was then published in book form at the end of March, going through seven editions by the following January. If Debussy was at all disconcerted by Louÿs's abrupt return to financial ease, he hid the fact well. But in adding his voice to what he called 'the European chorus of enthusiasm', in a letter of 10 April 1896 he allowed himself a criticism of the book which speaks eloquently of his own compositional concerns:

> Sometimes I feel the developments of your themes take on a value entirely of their own – the superb structure of the story is still there, but one is sad to lose sight of it with the rather abrupt incursion of over-rich material.

Debussy would sometimes claim, sardonically, that of course his music was without structure. But this was either in order to tease anyone who looked like analysing his works or to provide disingenuous support for those who insisted on calling him an Impressionist. In fact, as his comment in the above letter demonstrates, the interplay of structure and detail was to be a subject of his constant consideration – as, surely, for all great composers. Whether it was the difficulty of pruning Louÿs's over-rich material that prevented Debussy turning the novel into an opera, as he intended, we do not know. But certainly by 1900 Louÿs was more than a little irritated to find that, after he had turned down 'ten or twelve applications to authorize *Aphrodite* as an opera',[4] Debussy now withdrew his request for exclusive rights. At all events, Debussy's failure to set *Aphrodite* can stand as an exemplar of some forty unfinished or unstarted theatrical projects, including four based on literary works by Louÿs, which occupied him at various times between 1882 and 1917.[5]

In this context, his completion of *Pelléas et Mélisande* comes to seem almost as much of a miracle as the music itself. Both Louÿs and another friend, the violinist Eugène Ysaÿe, were anxious that *Pelléas* should see the light of day, Ysaÿe suggesting that Debussy should sanction the concert performance of excerpts – the traditional method in France of exciting interest among the capital's opera directors. Debussy refused point blank. The work was not built in such a way as to be cannibalized (which has not prevented one modern conductor from concocting a 'Pelléas symphony' that must have the composer spinning *prestissimo e furioso* in his grave). On the positive side, Debussy wrote to Ysaÿe that the *Three Nocturnes* were now scored for violin and orchestra and were, naturally, written for him to play.

For nearly three years after the Thérèse Roger affair in the spring of 1894, Debussy and Gaby seem to have lived more or less contentedly in their small apartment on the rue Gustave-Doré. Debussy's young friend René Peter, who had not seen the composer for some years, renewed contact with him around the middle of the 1890s:

> [Claude] was living under the sway of Gaby. She was a blonde with catlike eyes, a powerful chin and firm opinions. She looked after the domestic side – there was not much Mélisande in her – and that was quite a big undertaking, first of all because they were poor and secondly because Claude, being a large, spoilt child who refused to allow himself to be manhandled by life, indulged all his whims and was impervious to reason.
>
> Was he suddenly struck with the desire for that brown Japanese engraving which he later gave me for my birthday? He emptied his purse without stopping to think where the next day's dinner would come from. And while he was lost in thought in company with his genius, Gaby would be out raising money on knicknacks at some sordid pawnshop.

It is a well-documented phenomenon that men will often leave a domineering mother for an equally forceful wife or mistress. That partner, not surprisingly, comes to see herself as indispensable and, if this proves not to be the case, tends to respond in ways that cannot be misinterpreted. In February 1897 Debussy wrote to Louÿs:

> Gaby, she of the piercing eye, found a letter in my pocket which left no doubt as to the advanced state of a love affair, and containing enough picturesque material to inflame even the most stolid heart. Whereupon . . . Scenes . . . Tears . . . A real revolver and Le petit journal there to record it all . . . It's all senseless, pointless, and it changes absolutely nothing; you can't wipe out a mouth's kisses or a body's caresses by passing an india-rubber over them. Mind you, it'd be a handy invention, an india-rubber for removing adultery.

We do not know who the third party was, but at least Gaby cannot have been seriously hurt, since a month later Debussy was passing on to Louÿs 'her thanks and her best smile'. But we know too that Debussy's affection had lighted around this time on yet another woman, Catherine Stevens, the daughter of the Belgian painter Alfred Stevens, and that he even proposed marriage to her. In the words of Marcel Dietschy:

> with Pelléas finished, Debussy believed that he could have his work performed, if not in Paris, at least in Brussels or Ghent, and that he would become rich and be admitted de facto into the Stevens family circle. Nevertheless Catherine refused him, on the grounds that, 'Once Pelléas is performed, we will talk about it again!', as she said in her Notes . . . Her answer shows us, and this we should not forget, that Debussy, in certain social circles, then cut the figure of a Bohemian, of a glutton, of an 'eccentric' [un paradoxal], of a 'man without a penny' (all these expressions occur in Catherine Stevens's Notes); furthermore, his liaison with Gaby was held against him . . . one can understand that at the end of this century that made such a virtue of propriety, prudery and conventionality, young girls and their relatives were unable seriously to imagine a marriage with such a man.[6]

To call him a 'man without a penny' was not entirely fair, since the publisher Georges Hartmann had been subsidizing him from around 1894 to the tune of 6,000 francs a year, but Mlle Stevens's other attributions were close enough to the truth.

Work on the *Nocturnes* continued through the year and by Christmas Eve he had also completed the three *Chansons de Bilitis*, to prose poems by Pierre Louÿs – in quantity perhaps an insufficient substitute for his non-consummation of *Aphrodite*, but in quality a work any writer would be proud to have inspired.

In their report on *La damoiselle élue*, the Académie des Beaux-Arts had remarked on Debussy's ability to impart a poetical nature to a prose text. Effectively, he then did so again in his *Proses lyriques* in which his own texts, though set out (in the two which were published) as poems, are verse of the freest kind, barely distinguishable from prose except for the very occasional rhyme. The texts of the *Chansons de Bilitis* are in prose, but arranged in short paragraphs of from three to five lines which give credence to Louÿs's claim that they were translated by him for the first time from the Greek, as do the epigraphs from real Greek poets (Theocritus, Sappho, Philodemus) at the beginning of each of the three sections of the book.

This claim was in fact an out-and-out lie, as was the elaborate biographical sketch of the poetess which preceded them in the edition. In trying to make a fool of the learned experts, Louÿs was all too successful. One reviewer even took issue with the accuracy of his translations from the Greek! As Louÿs said later, 'for the critics I became a prankster and they withdrew their trust in me. The business with Bilitis had turned them sour.'[7] This *affaire* raises the intriguing question of whether Debussy, as one of Louÿs's closest friends at the time, was in on the secret. In fact, not everyone was taken in by the hoax, so it seems reasonable to assume that Debussy knew the translations were fakes.

This has no bearing, though, on the fact that Louÿs's prose poems are extremely beautiful and evocative, even if they evoke something that never existed. Here, we might say, are further examples of that

9   Debussy with Pierre Louÿs's Algerian mistress, Zohra, 1897

dreamlike scenario which Debussy had vaunted in his conversations
with Guiraud and subsequently found in *Pelléas et Mélisande*, and their
reference to a false reality, only loosely grounded in Louÿs's historical
knowledge, may well have given the composer a freedom he welcomed – for Louÿs's Asia Minor read Maeterlinck's Allemonde.

No verbal description can do justice to the extraordinary and individual beauty of these songs, which rank among Debussy's greatest
achievements. All that words can hope to do is to pinpoint his ambivalent attitude towards what he had written, and to attempt some kind of
explanation for it through the quotation of three passages of reminiscence.

The first, from his friend René Peter, tells us that Debussy had his
doubts about the decency of the Bilitis poems: 'he only just brought
himself', Peter says, 'on this front, to excuse [them], for their grace
and the frankness of their language . . . and even then, not all of them!'
When, in 1900, the young Blanche Marot was about to start rehearsing
the songs with the composer for their first public performance,
Debussy went to see her mother:

'Tell me, Madame, your daughter is not yet twenty? Good. It's very important, because if she understands the second song, "La chevelure", she won't sing it in the right way: she mustn't grasp the true brazenness of Bilitis's language...' My mother set Debussy's anxieties at rest and everything went splendidly.

In reality, Debussy was asking whether Blanche was a virgin (though see below, p. 96), and chaste sensuality runs through all three songs, developed possibly from the figure of the 'ange-femme' in *La damoiselle élue*. To modern sensibilities, Debussy's attitude may seem a touch creepy. Maybe he thought so too. His piano pupil Mme Gérard de Romilly recalled that at a small, private party organized by her at which the *Chansons* were to be heard, among other pieces,

> Debussy's music had a galvanic effect on an old Argentinian gentleman who had for some time been containing himself with difficulty. His outburst came immediately after hearing the *Chansons de Bilitis*. Not imagining for a moment that the composer was present, he marched up and down the room, shouting: 'No, no, that's not music! How do people come to write stuff like that?'
>
> We were all transfixed with embarrassment. I took him by the hand and led him up to Debussy, whom I introduced so as to put an end to his imprecations. Debussy was enchanted. He smiled and shook his hand and afterwards he would often ask me for news of this charming gentleman; and he would add, in his slightly nasal voice: 'I like that man, I should be delighted to see him again.'

Even though the charming gentleman's fury seems to have been directed against the music rather than the words, Debussy clearly relished the impact made by the combination of the two and may also, in his innermost heart, have welcomed having his doubts over the propriety of the texts confirmed from a respectable source. After all, his writings regularly dilate on the pernicious and deteriorating state of contemporary society (with Bilitis's make-believe world implicitly advanced as a better alternative). One thinks of Ravel, when a woman of advanced years was shouting 'Rubbish!' after a performance of *Boléro*, commenting, 'That old lady got the message!'[8] Both composers were intelligent enough to realize that a listener's perception of bad taste might just infer a corresponding perception of good taste – in which case that listener was to be courted. They were also, on a slightly lower level, enough in tune with the twentieth century to know that 'all publicity is good publicity'.

This question of publicity was one that now concerned Debussy deeply. The Paris public had heard no new work from him since the first performance of *Prélude à l'après-midi d'un faune* in December 1894 and by the summer of 1898 he was beset by creditors, despite Hartmann's regular subsidy. As he explained to his benefactor on 25 June,

> I hope to be able to calm the roaring of these gentlemen with the sum you're promising me; but then it'll be 'Settlement Day' and the same story over again. As I have no taste for prostitution, I'm wondering what trick I can use to dodge the hail of stones. The various lessons I rely on for my daily bread have gone off to the seaside, without a thought for my domestic economy, and the whole thing is a good deal more melancholy than all the *Ballades* of Chopin.

The lack of money and of performances contributed to making 1898 one of the most miserable years of Debussy's life. While the *Nocturnes* continued to give him problems, news reached him of the success of Fauré's incidental music for an English translation of Maeterlinck's *Pelléas et Mélisande* performed in London that June. Hartmann made the diplomatic error of saying he had enjoyed it; to which Debussy on 9 August responded by damning Fauré as 'the musical servant of a group of snobs and imbeciles' and claiming that he 'was commissioned to write the music by that English actress [Mrs Patrick Campbell] without being aware of the history of the project, and that subsequently he hasn't had the good manners to keep me informed'. In fact, as Edward Lockspeiser pointed out, Fauré must have known of Debussy's involvement, since Debussy had been granted the musical rights in the play by Maeterlinck. The plain truth is, the summer of 1898 found Debussy at his grumpiest and most bearlike.

Whether Gaby refused to countenance such behaviour, whether she caught Claude out in another affair or whether the financial struggle had simply become too much for her, by New Year's Day 1899, shortly after the composer's move 500 yards or so to another apartment in the rue Cardinet, she had left; and, for the moment, there was no one to take her place.

As if these problems were not enough, Debussy was now beginning to join the rest of French society in finding his life plagued by the Dreyfus Affair. Following Dreyfus's initial arrest in October 1894, the case had burned with varying intensities until, on 13 January 1898, Emile Zola published his famous article 'J'accuse' in the newspaper *L'aurore* and the 'Affair' was well and truly born. Pierre Louÿs soon sided with the anti-Dreyfusards, and this throws some light at least on a reference to the Affair in a letter he wrote to Debussy from Cairo two months later, on 23 March:

> Mon vieux, are you compromised to such an extent in the Dreyfus Affair that you no longer dare face me, or is it just that you're stewing day after day in voluptuous idleness?[9]

So was Debussy already a declared Dreyfusard? No evidence survives to support such a claim. But on 28 January 1899, a few weeks after Gaby left him, Debussy's name appeared with that of René Peter in the newspaper *Le temps* in support of a manifesto published in the same paper four days earlier, which declared:

> This is not an attempt to form a new league, but to bring together, by means of a joint declaration, the friends of legality and public order. The undersigned, deploring the repeated calls to illegality, violence and hatred, and in the conviction that at this time the duty of all Frenchmen is to work for reconciliation and appeasement . . . agree in stating that the current unrest, fatal as it is to the vital interests of the nation, cannot end unless all loyal citizens agree in advance to abide by the decision of the Court of Appeal, whatever that may be.

This, to my mind, still leaves Debussy's sympathies in doubt. Although one would expect him, from his past and current habits, to have been on the side of the underdog against the Establishment, his support for the manifesto can equally well be read as calling for 'a plague on both your houses'. The job of a government is to enforce the law, maintain order and support the struggling artist. For Debussy, as for Stravinsky, 'social disorder of any kind is primarily something which prevents him from doing his work – that is, fulfilling his duty. He hates disorder with all the strength of his egocentric nature'.[10]

Debussy continued working on the *Nocturnes* through the early months of 1899. Then, in April or perhaps a little earlier, he renewed acquaintance with a twenty-five-year-old mannequin in a fashionable clothes shop called Lilly Texier. His letter to her of 24 April makes the state of their relationship clear enough:

> My dear little Lili, Claude has still not recovered from the nibbles of your dear little mouth! And he can hardly leave off thinking of that evening when you gave him so much unexpected pleasure in the nicest way, and with the most complete abandon in the world.[11]

In that French way which the British find so curious, Gaby, far from regarding Lilly with a deadly hatred, became a close friend, even warning her of Claude's wandering eye – and, no doubt, other faults. A less than wholehearted respect for truth was, as we have seen, one of them; as when he assured Lilly on Saturday, 17 June that 'it is certain that *Pelléas et Mélisande* will be put on this winter and that from September my situation will improve very markedly'. In fact, although Debussy had played the score through to Albert Carré, the director of the Opéra-Comique, in May 1898, no production was to be even envisaged for another three years.

That letter was written between two events that were important for Debussy in their different ways. The previous Saturday, 10 June, his one-time friend Ernest Chausson was out bicycling with his daughter, ran into a wall and was killed. Debussy attended the funeral a few days later together with most of the cultural elite of Paris, including Degas, Rodin, de Régnier, Duparc, Fauré and Albéniz.[12] As Pierre Louÿs wrote to Mme Chausson, 'we always think there is time and that we will always see again those who are young' (Chausson was only forty-four). What were Debussy's thoughts on this melancholy occasion? Of that summer by the Marne? Of overheavy inner parts? Or of his own mortality, with the Nocturnes unfinished and Pelléas in limbo? And to have been seen publicly as one of a group of thirty or more creative artists all writing, painting, sculpting and composing, and all being read, seen and heard, except him . . .

Then a fortnight after Chausson's death, on Saturday 24 June, Pierre Louÿs married Louise, the daughter of the poet José-Maria de Hérédia. Debussy wrote a Wedding March (since lost) and was full of congratulations. But from this point the close friendship between the two slowly began to disintegrate. Maybe the continuing Dreyfus Affair played its part, but Debussy also commented on how strange it felt to be leaving his card (presumably, instead of just dropping in when he felt like it) while Louÿs for his part may have remembered (or his wife may have found?) a letter from Debussy of 9 February 1897 noting that he had 'made the acquaintance of M. José-Maria de Hérédia, which makes one more person to greet in the street and left me unmoved'.

In May, Debussy had intimated to Louÿs that his attachment to music prevented him thinking of marriage; in July, he described Lilly to Hartmann as 'marriageable'. On 19 October he acted on this latter judgement and three days later assured Hartmann that, as soon as the composer and his new wife had a table which would seat more than two people, he should be one of their first guests – from which it would appear that Hartmann's 6,000 francs a year were not being greatly supplemented from other quarters.

One of Debussy's last acts of the century was to finish the recalcitrant Nocturnes, which had occupied him certainly for the previous two years and perhaps for as long as the previous five. One of his first acts of the 1900s was, alas, to attend a rehearsal of Charpentier's opera Louise, which was premiered at the Opéra-Comique on 2 February. Louÿs had been at the premiere and had written that same evening to Debussy, complaining that, because he was in a box as somebody else's guest, etiquette had prevented him whistling (for which the hollow ends of

10 Claude and Lilly Debussy

Parisian house keys provided convenient instruments). Debussy replied four days later, with considerable force and at some length:

> It was a necessity, I think, for this work to be written, performed and applauded. It fills to perfection the need for vulgar beauty and imbecile art proclaimed by the many . . .
>
> Note how this man Charpentier takes the 'cries of Paris' (charming, natural, picturesque) and, like a filthy Prix de Rome winner, turns them into chlorotic cantilenas with harmonies which, to be polite, I'll call parasitic. Saints above, it's a thousand times more conventional than *Les Huguenots* and even uses the same means, without appearing to! And they call that 'Life'! Heavens, I'd rather drop dead on the spot. It's the sentimentality of a gentleman returning home around four in the morning and being moved to tears by the sight of the roadsweepers and the rag-and-bone men – and he thinks he can record the souls of the poor!!! . . .
>
> It's a question more of stupidity than of evil intentions; only people don't like beauty because it's a nuisance and doesn't accommodate itself to their nasty little souls. Many more works like *Louise* and there'll be no hope of pulling them out of the mud.

The vigour of Debussy's expostulations can perhaps best be explained with reference to performances of two of his own works in March and August of that year. On 17 March, Blanche Marot gave the first performance of the *Chansons de Bilitis*, accompanied by the composer; and on 23 August, as part of one of the concerts to mark the Universal Exhibition, she sang the name part in *La damoiselle élue*. Clearly, Debussy felt the atmospheres of the two works were to some extent linked. On 24 May, writing to Marot about her part in the generally well-received performance of *La damoiselle*, he enthused: 'At times, you were able to escape so totally from the material environment, it became other-worldly . . .' Whatever *Louise* may be, other-worldly it is not. And behind Debussy's denunciation of its 'slices of life' lay also a full decade of immersion in Symbolist attitudes and ideals.

At the same time, Blanche Marot's status as the virgin who did not understand what she was singing about in 'La chevelure' (see p. 90), or as the 'ange/femme', cannot really be justified, since we now know that at the time of the first performance of *Chansons de Bilitis* she was the mistress of Debussy's benefactor Georges Hartmann, and Debussy certainly knew this too. A solution to the problem could be that Debussy went to see her mother some time before the performance and that she and Hartmann formed their liaison in the interim. But for our understanding of Debussy's mentality, the crucial point is that she was obviously able to sing the song *as though* not understanding it (otherwise he would surely have cancelled the concert), and without the knowingness he found so repugnant in *Louise* – and which, incidentally, Poulenc later detested in singers of his own songs. There is, therefore, no requirement to label the *Chansons* 'for virgins only'.

With that first performance and with the privilege of being one of the composers chosen to represent France in the Universal Exhibition (even though the committee's discussion on the point was apparently lively), Debussy's stock would seem at last to have been rising once more. But two sad events now clouded his horizons. First, on 23 April, Georges Hartmann died suddenly at the age of fifty-seven. His agreement with Debussy had, apparently, been only on a gentlemanly footing and his nephew and heir soon made it clear that not only was the annual sum of 6,000 francs ceasing forthwith, but the sums already paid were loans, not gifts, and would have to be returned. Then Lilly became pregnant; and in a Paris clinic, the Maison Dubois, where she stayed between 14 and 23 August, the child was aborted 'pour les plus misérables raisons', in the words of Marcel Dietschy.[13] The day Lilly came home from the clinic, 23 August, was indeed a busy day for the composer, since it was on that afternoon that *La damoiselle* was performed at the Trocadéro.

Debussy wrote to Louÿs on 25 August:

> Lilly . . . was operated on several days ago, but that's not all; it seems her body in general is in a poor state and (between ourselves) she has tubercular patches at the top of both lungs. We are having to take immediate steps to deal with these, namely sending her to the Pyrenees for three or four months! You can imagine what a torment it's all been, quite apart from my financial situation, desperate as usual! I don't know any more how to cope with so many contradictory events.

Did Lilly ever get to the Pyrenees, or was this one of Claude's *fantaisies?* Certainly she was not absent for anything like three or four months, since on 11 October Debussy concluded a letter from Paris to Louÿs by saying 'my wife would like you to embrace yours while assuring her of her warmest friendship'.[14]

But the great news of the last months of 1900 was that the three *Nocturnes* were scheduled to be performed by the Lamoureux Orchestra under their conductor Camille Chevillard on 9 December. In the event no female chorus was available, so only the first two were given. In general the critics were favourable and one or two others in the musical world were even ecstatic, like Mme de Saint-Marceaux and the pianist Ricardo Viñes. Ravel was there too and the next few years seemed to have been those in which the two composers, though never intimate friends, were closest to each other. At some point during 1900, Ravel had been allowed to attend a private performance of *Pelléas* and in April 1901 he was embarking on a transcription of the unheard third piece, 'Sirènes', of the 'admirable' *Nocturnes* for two pianos with Raoul Bardac, later to be Debussy's stepson.[15] Interestingly, Debussy and Ravel found common ground in praising Liszt's *Faust Symphony* which was also on the 9 December programme: Debussy calling it, in a letter of three days earlier, 'food and drink for a whole generation of composers, and a lesson in orchestration too', and Ravel 'this astonishing symphony in which there appear (written earlier and, what's more, so much better orchestrated) the most striking themes of the *Ring*'.

Among the positive critiques in the press, none can have pleased Debussy so much as the one in the February 1901 issue of the *Revue hebdomadaire* by his friend Paul Dukas.[16] Dukas was known by everyone to be a scrupulously honest critic for whom friendship was no passport to good notices and he used his friendship with Debussy not as an excuse for flattery, but as an opportunity for understanding. He also went a good deal further in his references than the *Nocturnes* themselves. Since Debussy confessed that he was filled with pride by the review, reminding Dukas that 'to have intelligence at the service of complete understanding is a luxury you're used to', it deserves a brief discussion as a marker of Debussy's position at the start of the new century.

The notice begins with Dukas explaining that Debussy has made life difficult for himself by refusing to repeat his own past formulae: 'none of his works appears as the expected consequence of another; they all bring something special which denotes, if not an absolute transformation of his manner, at least a different and unexpected point of view'. After commenting that in his settings of Verlaine and Baudelaire 'his task seems to be to note down the most distant harmonics of the poetry', he concludes his general remarks on Debussy's music with these evocative words:

> Most of his compositions are therefore symbols of symbols, but expressed in a language in itself so rich and so persuasive that at

times it attains the eloquence of a new word, bearing within itself its own law, and often far more intelligible than the language of the poems on which it is based. Such is the case, for example, with L'après-midi d'un faune.

Of the two Nocturnes, Dukas insisted that 'Nuages' was not strictly 'meteorological' but that its musical elements were, 'so to speak, volatilized in the ether of the symbol', while 'Fêtes' suggested to him a celebration seen in a dream. Of the two, he preferred 'Nuages', 'perhaps less because of the music itself than because the art that truly belongs to M. Debussy appears to me there more distinctly drawn'.

Well might Debussy be proud to have so much truth proclaimed so succinctly and so openly: in particular that he had now established the 'musique à moi' which he had dreamt of over a decade before, and that listeners would have to get used to the idea of his music changing with every piece – an outbreak of hopefulness on Dukas' part, because Debussy was to stay at least one step ahead of most of his audiences until his death.

Looking back at Debussy's career during the 1890s, one gets the impression of a slow but persistent pressure building up that finally catapulted him to fame and notoriety with Pelléas et Mélisande. At the time Debussy himself barely felt this, or only occasionally. The overall tone of his letters during this decade is resigned and angry, despite the flights of humour and idealism, and at one especially low point in 1898 he obviously talked to Louÿs about the temptations of suicide. To him the change in his situation, when it did come, must have seemed quite sudden. But the fact that he had represented France at the International Exhibition, that the Nocturnes, for all their strangeness, had impressed the critics and that L'après-midi, whether or not you thought it effete and unwholesome, had now begun to take on the air almost of a classic – against all this, the fulminations of a Saint-Saëns could no longer hold the field.

The first small upward step was decidedly not his involvement as provider of incidental music for a mimed presentation of some of

Louÿs's *Chansons de Bilitis* in February, in which antiquity was an excuse for a frank display of feminine charms, but rather his appointment to be the music critic of *La revue blanche*. It was indeed only a small step, in that the review could not be said to have been respectable or of the Establishment. Its editor, Félix Fénéon, had been rounded up in the anti-anarchist purges of 1894 and, when acquitted with the help of Mallarmé's testimony, had gone on to promote his strong Dreyfusard opinions in the revue. Whether Debussy's money problems, by 1901 becoming acute, would ever have led him to write for an anti-Dreyfus magazine must remain a matter of conjecture, but certainly *La revue blanche*, apart from paying him money, was a useful outlet for his ideas. Its literary contributors had included Verlaine, Mallarmé, Jules Laforgue, de Régnier and Mendès and would later include Alfred Jarry and Marinetti, the Italian Futurist. But acquiring Debussy was quite a *coup* since, as Richard Langham Smith notes, 'compared with the other columns, the magazine's music criticism lagged far behind, hardly living up to its otherwise progressive outlook. Thus the composer Debussy merited the bold type accorded him on the cover of the first issue containing his column'.

This was the issue of 1 April. Although the subjects of his review were really four musical items, including Schumann's *Scenes from Faust* and the third act of *Siegfried*, he not unnaturally began with a profession of faith:

> This column will contain sincere and truly felt impressions rather than criticism, since the latter too often resembles brilliant variations on the tune 'You're wrong not to do the same as me', or 'You're talented, I'm not, this can't be allowed to continue any longer . . .' I shall aim to descry, through the works themselves, the manifold movements which have brought them into being and whatever they contain of inner life. Does this not offer an interest, even if a different one from the game which consists of taking works to pieces like curious watches?

The eight reviews Debussy contributed to *La revue blanche* between April and December 1901 are unfailingly lively and often provocative, which was presumably what Fénéon was after. When Debussy doesn't like something, he says so – in Schumann's *Scenes from Faust*, for example, he complains that one is always tripping over Mendelssohn, 'that elegant, facile notary' (Ravel would not have agreed with him there!). Elsewhere some of his enthusiasms were uncommon in the Paris of the time. Musorgsky's *The Nursery*, for instance:

> No one has spoken to what is best in us more tenderly and more profoundly; he is unique and will remain so thanks to his art which is without rules, without desiccating formulae . . . All these stories are noted down, I must point out, with an extreme simplicity; Musorgsky needs only a chord which would seem impoverished to M. . . . (I've forgotten his name!) or a modulation so instinctive that it would seem strange to M. . . . (the same man!).

In his third article, of 1 May, he tried to relay to his readers the emotions roused in him by what he called 'the primitives, Palestrina, Vittoria, Orlando di Lasso', who, he said,

> made use of that divine 'arabesque'. They discovered the principle in Gregorian chant and supported its delicate intertwinings with firm counterpoint. When Bach took over the arabesque he made it more supple and fluid and, despite the severe discipline that great master imposed on Beauty, it was able to move with that free, ever fresh fantasy which still amazes us today.

Whether Debussy's idea of the 'arabesque' came from Mallarmé or Ruskin or painters such as Maurice Denis, who designed the cover for the score of *La damoiselle élue*, it was to preoccupy him until the end of his life. As for Bach, Debussy was still playing piano duet versions of the organ works as late as 1894 and many of his writings, in articles and letters, expatiate on the problem Bach had been able to solve, of how to hide an astonishing technique beneath a surface of simplicity and grace. It may indeed have been Debussy's own failure to do this that prompted him to abandon his projected set of five songs called *Nuits blanches*, written to his own words and intended as a complement to the *Proses lyriques*. The recently discovered autographs of the first two reveal him going through the motions but failing to strike a note of true authority. Also he may have had to admit to himself that, as a Symbolist prose writer, he was not in Maeterlinck's class and that his settings reflected the fact.

After his first few articles in *La revue blanche*, Debussy seems to have come to the conclusion (or perhaps one or two snappish readers brought him to it) that speaking his mind so openly might be counter-productive. He therefore invented a character, M. Croche, as a mouth-piece for his more outrageous statements. M. Croche made his entrance on 1 July and his first target was Wagner:

> I remember the parallel he drew between Beethoven's orchestra, represented for him by a black and white pattern which as a result gave the exquisite range of greys, and Wagner's: a sort of multi-coloured resin smeared on almost uniformly, in which he told me he could no longer distinguish the sound of a violin from that of a trombone.

Debussy's love affair with Wagner of the mid-1880s had gradually turned sour over the next fifteen years and his feelings were to remain confused for the following fifteen. Much of the musical public, how-ever, was still in thrall and did not care to see its hero vilified. *Tannhäuser* for example, introduced to the Opéra in May 1895, had just reached its 100th performance in November 1900.

If getting the music critic's post on *La revue blanche* was a small step up in Debussy's career, a giant leap occurred on 3 May 1901 when Debussy at last received official confirmation from Albert Carré, the director of the recently built Opéra-Comique in the rue Favart, that *Pelléas et Mélisande* would be given there the following season. Apart from the first performance of the complete *Nocturnes* on 27 October, at which 'Sirènes' was greeted with some whistling (the female chorus was apparently a little out of tune), the rest of the year was devoted to re-orchestrating his opera. Then, on 29 December, the cast list for *Pelléas* was announced in *Le ménestrel* . . . and Debussy's troubles began.

5 Idol and victim (1902–1907)

Rehearsals for *Pelléas* began at the Opéra-Comique on 13 January with Jean Périer as Pelléas and the twenty-five-year-old Scottish soprano Mary Garden as Mélisande. Maeterlinck had hoped that the role would go to his mistress Georgette Leblanc and, when this hope was thwarted, moved on to the attack, claiming that the permission to set his play he had given Debussy in a letter of 19 October 1895 did not remove from the dramatist the right to be consulted over casting. In February he even took the composer to law. But in the end, like the characters in his play, he had to bow to destiny; though with a bad grace and a hope that the opera would be 'an immediate and resounding flop'.[1]

Subsequent recordings by Leblanc suggest that her voice was really too large and voluptuous for the role (although she did sing it in Boston in 1912). Mary Garden might seem to have had the wrong credentials since she first came to public notice as a last-minute substitute in the name part of the despised *Louise* in 1900, but Debussy sensed in her a remoteness that fitted his conception of a *princesse lointaine*: as he said to her, on learning she came from Aberdeen, 'To think that you had to come from the cold far North to create my Mélisande . . .' We may also note that in Mélisande's monologue that opens Act III he quotes melodically from Ariel's song 'Where the bee sucks' in Chausson's *The Tempest* – another memory of that concert on 2 February 1889 when Debussy's music was first heard at the

Société nationale and, no less importantly, an indication of an un-
spoken liaison in his mind between Ariel and Mélisande, free spirits
both.

Before individual rehearsals began, Debussy played through the
whole opera to the cast in the conductor Messager's house. Fifty years
later, Garden recalled:

> There we sat in the drawing room – M. Carré and M. and Mme
> Messager and the whole cast – each of us with a score, heads bowed
> as if we were all at prayer. While Debussy played I had the most
> extraordinary emotions I have ever experienced in my life. Listening
> to that music I seemed to become someone else, someone inside of
> me whose language and soul were akin to mine. When Debussy got
> to the fourth act I could no longer look at my score for the tears. It was
> all very strange and unbearable. I closed my book and just listened to
> him, and as he played the death of Mélisande, I burst into the most
> awful sobbing, and Mme Messager began to sob along with me, and
> both of us fled into the next room. I shall never forget it. There we
> were crying as if we had just lost our best friend, crying as if nothing
> would console us again.[2]

Throughout the fifteen weeks of rehearsal the resonances of that
impact sustained the cast through an intensive schedule: on 27
January the conductor Messager took part for the first time; on 8
March the first read-through for the orchestra (faulty parts not helping); on 23 March, singers and orchestra work on the first three acts;
on 7 April, first complete rehearsal; on 17 April, 'Messager in a rage,
bellowing at the orchestra and poor Périer'; on 28 April, dress
rehearsal; on 30 April, premiere. The composer not only attended
sixty-nine rehearsal sessions but, in the last four weeks before the premiere, had to extend several of the orchestral interludes to allow time
for changing the scenery. Well might he write to Carré in March:
'Please forgive me for not replying at once to your charming and . . .
helpful letter. In this life of mine like a machine with steam up, civility
disappears but friendship remains (at 58 rue Cardinet).'

Henri Busser, who conducted the offstage chorus of sailors on the first night and took over from Messager on the fourth, has left us some telling souvenirs of the opera's early life:

> 28 April: The great day finally arrives! Public dress rehearsal of *Pelléas*. Success is assured with the fourth and fifth acts. Debussy takes refuge in Messager's office and nervously smokes one cigarette after another.

> 30 April [? 1 May]: The morning after the premiere I go to see Debussy in his modest apartment on the rue Cardinet: he's writing interludes to join some of the scenes together . . . This little room we're in, with oil paintings, watercolours and drawings on the walls, radiates happiness. The delightful Lilly is its source. She's happy that *Pelléas* is being produced. 'It's my work too', she says, 'because I gave Claude encouragement when he was despairing of ever seeing his work reach the stage!'

> 3 May: Third performance. Large audience, more responsive and sympathetic. At the end there are calls for Debussy, but he refuses to appear on stage . . . Debussy is well aware that he has broken completely with the pernicious habits of opera composers. He tells us: 'I try and move the listener through the simplicity of the vocal line, through the discretion of the orchestra; I detest the brutal effects so greatly prized by my predecessors.'

> 8 May: Debussy and his wife come to see me and put me on my guard against the possible whims of the singers. Both of them seem quite exhausted.

> 26 June: Fourteenth performance of *Pelléas* which, to my great regret, is the last one this season. The audience very enthusiastic. Three or four curtain calls after each act.

Busser's statement in his entry for 3 May, 'large audience, more responsive and sympathetic', implies truthfully that the dress rehearsal and the first two performances had had their problems. At the dress rehearsal, the audience were surprised to be handed a 'programme du spectacle' which gave a salaciously slanted résumé of the plot: 'Pelléas, Golaud's brother, takes a walk with his little sister-in-law in the shade of the garden. Ho, Ho . . .' Mary Garden was quite sure that Maeterlinck was responsible for this pamphlet, even though its authorship has never been established beyond doubt. Further audience unease was provoked by Garden's foreign accent – for example, when she sang 'Je n'ai pas de *curages* [*courage*]', '*curages*' being the dirt that gets stuck in drains – and by Yniold's repeated phrase 'petit père' in Act III scene 4.

The audience could be split roughly into three groups: the general public, the critics and Establishment musical figures, and the young Turks together with a few enlightened *mélomanes*. The reaction of the general public is the hardest to gauge, since newspaper critics cannot always be relied upon to distinguish their own opinion from that of the auditorium as a whole. The best indicator is perhaps the financial receipts. If one excepts the first night, on which many of the tickets were given to the press or other people of influence, the receipts for the next three performances (on 2, 3 and 8 May) totalled 3,938. 50 francs, 5,981 francs and 7,364 francs respectively.[3] Apart from the first performance and the tenth, which was a matinée, all of them made a profit. More significantly for determining the general public's attitude, the takings for four performances (nos. 3–7) which were on subscribers' nights were on average no higher than those given over entirely to the public. We must conclude that the public liked the opera, or at least was intrigued by it.

From the critics we have almost too much evidence. The music was 'sickly and practically lifeless', the composer was tied to a system which involved 'sacrificing music to vague conceptions and dangerous compromises' (between what, we are not told), while 'rhythm, song and tonality are three things unknown to M. Debussy and deliberately scorned by him'. Some critics were more enlightened and one has to doff one's hat to Gustave Bret, for example, then assistant organist to Widor at St Sulpice, who wrote in *La presse*:

> This music takes you over, it penetrates into you by the strength of
> an art which I admire more than I understand. From one end to the

other, the word-setting is extremely sober, but one does not lose
a word of it. The orchestra is infinitely discreet, producing the
strangest and most exquisite sonorities. No outbreaks of violence,
no *éclat*. Nothing but materials of utter probity.

But Bret was only twenty-six years old, and so really belongs rather
to the third group of students, like Ravel, Inghelbrecht, Maurice
Delage and Léon-Paul Fargue, together with music-lovers like Mme
de Saint-Marceaux. The students packed the stuffy, overheated upper
balconies, some of them like Ravel for every one of the fourteen performances of the first run, taking every opportunity to express their
enthusiasm. Let the young writer Jacques Rivière speak for them all:

> People do not perhaps realize well enough what *Pelléas* was for the
> young audience who greeted it at its birth, for those who were sixteen
> to twenty when it first appeared: a miraculous world, a cherished
> paradise where we could escape from all our troubles . . . I say this
> not as a metaphor: *Pelléas* was for us a particular forest, a particular
> region and a terrace overlooking a particular sea. We would find
> refuge there, knowing the secret door, and the outside world had
> no more hold upon us.[4]

This appeal to the younger element in the audience obviously had
implications for the future.

In the autumn, rehearsals for a revival of the opera took up much of
Debussy's time. Otherwise his only project seems to have been a
version of *As You Like It* with the poet and novelist Paul-Jean Toulet,
returning to an idea he had had as a student in Rome – in the 1889
questionnaire he named Rosalind as his favourite heroine. No music
for the project survives and it is hard, as often with Debussy, to know
exactly how frivolous he was being when he suggested to Toulet in
October that Orlando's wrestling match might be accompanied by a
chorus of 'He's done for!', 'No, he's not!' sung off-stage by the
Chanteurs de Saint-Gervais!

The New Year of 1903 saw Debussy finally and openly accepted by
the Establishment with his promotion to Chevalier of the Légion

11 *Pelléas et Mélisande* Act III scene 3; on the terrace after emerging from the dungeons

d'Honneur. As René Peter recalled, this gave pleasure in many quarters:

> The morning after Debussy had been made a member of the Légion d'Honneur, he put a light overcoat on top of the ribbon and hailed a cab to go to the corner of the suburbs where his father lived. Debussy *père* was standing out on the lawn of his tiny garden in his shirtsleeves, a waxing brush in his right hand, his left inside a large shoe which he was polishing. As he didn't see his son at first, Debussy gave a loud cough.
>
> 'Ah, my dear boy, what a nice surprise!'
>
> That was not the end of the surprises, for Claude came towards his

father and, without saying anything, briskly opened his overcoat. His father too was speechless; he stood stock still, looking dazed and pale; two large tears, nourished by twenty years of disappointment, rolled down his cheeks and into his moustache before he could recover himself. Then suddenly he embraced Claude in a frenzy of love.

'Ah, my boy! My boy!'

. . . while the back of the new *chevalier* was subjected to furious, repeated blows from the ecstatic brush and the grateful shoe. Claude loved telling this story.

'You see', he said . . ., 'in that brief moment I could feel pride at having been good for something.'

Debussy seems to have completed no music in the first half of 1903, though he may have been sketching out ideas for *The Devil in the Belfry*, a planned 'musical tale' in two acts based on the Poe short story. One reason was that he now returned to writing regular musical criticism, as a weekly contributor to the daily newspaper *Gil Blas*, writing no fewer than twenty-four articles between 12 January and 28 June with Colette as his critical colleague. Richard Langham Smith, in publishing their reviews side by side, comments that 'reading between the lines one feels that the two approaches had a good deal in common' and that Colette's 'ideals of criticism, though less lofty, are basically similar: both writers wish to be themselves, to preserve their immediate reactions and to place them at the centre of their writings about the arts'.

Debussy's articles contain much that was to become familiar from his pen over the years. Wagner was a bad model for the French and Gluck had been a disaster for French music, all the more because he drove Rameau into the shadows. He supports the idea of a popular theatre, with free seats for all, somewhat against the run of his elitist creed of ten years earlier, and puts forward an ideal of music in the open air; in both, his targets include the traditional buildings which induce respect and even fear rather than a true response to the works performed in them.

Grieg's Piano Concerto and Mendelssohn's Reformation Symphony get the thumbs down, as do Alfred Cortot's intrusive lock of hair and extravagant gestures while conducting *Parsifal*. In criticizing his senior compatriots he is a touch more diplomatic. Over a revival of *Werther* he points out Massenet's realization that

> despite the jealousy of the men, his faithful band of beautiful lady listeners still preserved for him the same passion . . . Perhaps they were reminded by this music of those moments when their beauty had been enhanced by being divinely moved? You may be sure such things do not go unremembered.

Two prophetic pleas are worth noting among the jokes and lively metaphors. In an article on the Prix de Rome, Debussy suggests that women should be allowed to enter; and in his last article he asked that some opportunity be found for putting on Russian opera. Both these ideas were realized within the following decade.

But in early July Debussy gave up his *Gil Blas* column and followed the pattern of the previous three years, joining Lilly in spending several months with her parents at Bichain in Normandy. It was here that he wrote the first group of piano pieces to explore the new world of sound opened up by *L'après-midi*, the *Nocturnes* and *Pelléas*. The titles of the three *Estampes* take us a long way from the bourgeois salon: in 'Pagodes' to the Far East, as imagined by Debussy through his memories of the gamelan players at the 1889 Exhibition, in 'La soirée dans Grenade' to the sounds of the sultry Spanish night, and in 'Jardins sous la pluie' upstairs into the nursery with its echoes of the composer's favourite song 'Nous n'irons plus au bois' (We shall to the wood no more) and the lullaby 'Do, do, l'enfant do'. Is the child of the household looking through the window down at the rain-drenched garden? It is tempting to think so, since six years later in 1909 Debussy was telling an interviewer: 'Only souls without imagination go to the country for inspiration. I can look into my garden and find there everything that I want.'[5]

For once, Debussy worked fast and by August was already about to send the proofs back to his new publisher Jacques Durand, who was to

12 Emma Bardac, June 1904

bring out most of his music from now on. 'You'll have to return to your piano practice', he told Durand,

> if you don't want to make these nightmare *Estampes* more melancholy still by your somewhat wanton inexactitude. I'm working at *La mer* ... If God is kind to me, I'll be a good way through by the time I return.

In the event God was not kind to him, or at least not in that way, and *La mer* was to take him another eighteen months. Before leaving Bichain, he had at least decided on working titles for its three movements, although his self-confidence did not extend to satisfying Lilly by buying a house in the area.

Their marriage remained outwardly happy. But after four years her gentleness, naivety and simplicity were beginning to lose their attraction, unsupported as they were by any real musical or intellectual abilities. In other circumstances the marriage might have lasted. But shortly after his return to Paris on 1 October his pupil Raoul Bardac asked him to dinner with his mother Emma, who, in addition to being an accomplished singer, had a decade earlier been Fauré's mistress and the dedicatee of his song cycle *La bonne chanson*. Through that autumn and the early months of 1904, the friendship between Debussy and Emma Bardac grew into something stronger. Raoul Bardac's sister, Dolly de Tinan, told me that he always felt guilty at having introduced Debussy to his mother, but we know from Mme Bardac's first husband that matters were not easy between them and that she always had an eye open for artistic celebrities. He thought that because he had the money, she would always come back to him: in Debussy's case, he was wrong.

On 9 January 1904, the Spanish pianist Ricardo Viñes gave the first performance of the *Estampes* at a Société nationale concert in the Salle Erard and 'Jardins sous la pluie' was encored. But the pleasure of this success was considerably attenuated by an article in *Le journal* on 22 January signed 'Jean Lorrain'. As François Lesure says, the sort of attack it contained was not to be expected by Debussy from someone with whom he shared mutual friends. But an attack it indubitably was, on Debussy's music and on the in-group Lorrain calls the 'Pelléastres':

> Convulsed with admiration for the sunny pizzicatos of that little masterpiece *L'après-midi d'un faune*, they made it a categorical imperative to swoon at the studied dissonances in *Pelléas*'s long recitatives. The irritation provoked by those prolonged chords and by those interminable beginnings of phrases which had been introduced a hundred times; that sensual titillation, exasperating and ultimately cruel, imposed on the ear by the growth of a theme which is interrupted a hundred times and never gets to the end; all this . . . gathered support from an audience of snobs and *poseurs*.[6]

Though dissuaded by Pierre Louÿs from replying, Debussy was hurt: it was his first taste of the double edge of fame, teaching him that an idol in one camp can simultaneously be a victim in another.

Meanwhile he finished his *Trois chansons de France* to two texts by the fifteenth-century poet Charles d'Orléans and one by the seventeenth-century Tristan Lhermite. Just as he was happy to invent his own sub-style to evoke a bogus ancient Asia Minor in the *Bilitis* songs, so here he makes no attempt to distinguish between the fifteenth and seventeenth centuries. By and large the harmonies of all three songs are simpler and more firmly anchored to traditional tonal pillars than in the Bilitis songs and the textures are less arrestingly original. Since the set, published in May 1904, is dedicated to Mme S. Bardac, it is tempting to try to read a biographical message into the composer's choice of poems and perhaps even into that of the musical style. Any such attempt appears doomed by the text of the third song 'Pour que Plaisance est morte' (Because Pleasure is dead, this May I am dressed in black). But the music is sad in the most delicate, almost pretty manner. Did 'Plaisance' represent Debussy's past life of what he now felt to have been superficial delights? Certainly in the second song, 'La grotte', we must be struck by Debussy's setting of the central verse:

> These waves, weary from their exertions,
> As they forced their way over the gravel bed,
> Have come to rest now in this pool
> Where in time past Narcissus died . . .

Leaving aside the question of who Narcissus might be in this context, we are surely meant to respond to the music's sudden settling into a calm E major for the third line.

By May, Debussy's friendship with Louÿs had come to an end. Almost simultaneously another friendship took its place, with a thirty-year-old musician and scholar called Louis Laloy. This same year Laloy received a doctorate for his thesis on 'Aristoxenus of Tarentum and the Music of Antiquity'; and if this seems an unlikely basis for a friendship with the forty-two-year-old Claude, no further support is provided by the fact that he was still a pupil of d'Indy at the Schola Cantorum and that he came to Debussy's notice through his published analysis of the first four bars of *Pelléas* . . . But Laloy was to remain close to the composer until his death, as well as writing the first biography of the composer in French.

Whether or not his friendship with the scholarly Laloy encouraged Debussy to focus on the musical past, he interpreted his next commission in what might loosely be called a 'neoclassical' fashion. It came

from the director of the instrument makers Pleyel who wanted to promote their new chromatic harp, which had two rows of strings slanted
across each other, one for 'white' notes, the other for 'black', and
Debussy obliged with *Danse sacrée et danse profane* for harp and string
orchestra. The first of these, based on a theme by Francesco de
Lacerda, follows Debussy's habit of interpreting 'sacred' through
consecutive common chords, sometimes modal, sometimes chromatic: the effect is orderly and hieratic – gone the free, floating
sensuality of *L'après-midi* or of the *Bilitis* songs.

By contrast, in the months from June to August Debussy's domes-
tic life was turned upside down. It is clear that by June, if not before, he
and Emma had become lovers. On 15 July he packed Lilly off alone to
Bichain and the next day sent her a letter, saying 'for some time I've
been worried that I'm going round the same circle of ideas. Now that I
seem to have found a new direction, that's why I dare not let go of it,
whatever it costs me.' Over the following weeks Debussy gradually
hinted more and more clearly to Lilly as to the way things were likely to
go. Then, at the end of July, he and Emma left for Jersey, going on to
Pourville. There was one, painful, meeting with Lilly on 13 September,
but when Debussy returned definitively to the capital at the end of the
month it was to set up house on his own. At least four times Lilly
threatened to commit suicide. On Thursday 13 October she shot herself in the breast, the bullet passing twice through the stomach –
maybe she was unable to face their fifth wedding anniversary in six
days' time. Mary Garden went to see her in the clinic on the rue
Blomet:

> They took me into a tiny room, and there lay Lilly, with a bullet in her
> breast, wanting to die because her Claude had not come back to her.
> You must understand that this young girl never knew anything else in
> life but her love of Debussy. She took care of him like a child. They
> had worries and debts and disappointments, but nobody ever got
> into the little apartment of the rue Cardinet to interrupt Debussy at
> his music . . . When Lilly had finished telling me the story, the
> surgeon came in to dress her wound . . . and opened her nightdress,

and in my life I have never seen anything so beautiful as Lilly Debussy from the waist up. It was just like a glorious marble statue, too divine for words! Debussy had always said to me, 'Mary, there's nothing in the world like Lilly's body.' Now I knew what he meant.

And lying underneath Lilly's left breast was a round dark hole where the bullet had gone in, without touching anything vital – and Lilly didn't die. They never got the bullet out. That little token of her love for Claude Debussy stayed with her till she died, and that was in 1932.

In the three months of June to August, Debussy had put the finishing touches to two works, the piano pieces *Masques* and *L'isle joyeuse* as well as composing the second set of *Fêtes galantes* to poems by Verlaine; all three were published in September, but the songs had their first performance before publication, on 23 June. The third and last song, 'Colloque sentimental', Debussy's farewell to the poet, sounds also like a farewell to Lilly as the two ghostly lovers converse: 'How blue was the sky, and great our hope!' 'Hope, crushed, has fled toward the black sky.'

For the next six months Debussy's energies were spent in three directions: in completing the score of *La mer* (finally achieved on 5 March 1905), in continuing his affair with Emma (by March she was two months pregnant) and in haggling with Lilly over a divorce settlement (by March she was still insisting she wanted to live with him). In May Debussy was still arguing with her through lawyers until, on 2 August, the divorce was finalized.

The desperate interplay of musical and marital concerns is nowhere more graphically displayed than in a small notebook[7] which contains in pencil both sketches for *La mer* and details of his grounds for the divorce. The latter make melancholy reading:

Anger – even in front of her family – violence with the servants;
quarrels about money . . .; lies of every kind . . .; constant
dissimulation – my friends, for example, never liked – was only after
a slightly better *situation* – she made a mistake there and avenged
herself by exercising a daily tyranny over my thoughts and dealings

...; ... If Mme D had been an honest person, it is probable that my friends would not have been so attentive to her – !!

Those two exclamation marks, added in blue, tell the bitter truth. Many of his friends now deserted him, including René Peter, Paul Dukas and André Messager. Pierre Louÿs and Ravel contributed to a fund for Lilly. It seems that only Laloy, Jacques Durand and Satie remained on good terms with him. 'Was there some debt to life I had to repay?' he asked in a letter of 14 April to Laloy. 'I don't know ... but often I had to smile in case people suspected I might be about to burst into tears.'

If Paris that summer seemed hostile and unforgiving, abroad Debussy's music had slowly begun to make a mark. In Germany, Busoni had conducted the first performance of *L'après-midi* with the Berlin Philharmonic on 5 November 1903 and there were at least four more performances of the work over the next couple of years; Vienna heard it first on 8 February 1905. Busoni and the Berlin Philharmonic had also given the first German performance of 'Nuages' and 'Fêtes' on 1 December 1904. In London, Henry Wood conducted the first British performance of *L'après-midi* on 20 August 1904 at a Promenade Concert – one of two novelties in the programme of which 'neither proved very interesting'.[8]

Russia was even less responsive. D'Indy conducted *L'après-midi* twice at Pavlovsk in July 1904, both without success; the conductor was unflustered, saying 'It's no matter. They'll get there one day.'[9] A few months earlier 'Rimsky[-Korsakov]'s guests on his sixtieth birthday [18 March n.s.] heard, and ridiculed, Debussy's *Estampes* – the host disliked the Frenchman's music as much as his most famous pupil [Stravinsky] liked it.'[10] But at least the guests had the opportunity of hearing the *Estampes*, less than ten weeks after Viñes had given their first performance in Paris.

In the summer of 1905 Debussy, like the rest of musical Paris, was entertained by the *affaire Ravel* when the thirty-year-old composer was eliminated in the preliminary round of the Prix de Rome competition, leading to angry comments in the press and elsewhere. In July and August he and Emma had a holiday (though correcting the proofs of *La mer* and finishing the first set of piano *Images* were also on the agenda) at the Grand Hotel, Eastbourne where, he told Durand, 'the sea unfurls itself with an utterly British correctness. In the foreground is a well-groomed lawn on which little chips off important, imperialist blocks are rushing around.'

October 1905 was one of the busiest months of Debussy's entire life. First, he and Emma rented a house at 80 avenue du Bois de Boulogne (now avenue Foch) and moved in. Then he was immersed in rehearsals for the first performance of *La mer*, to be conducted by Camille Chevillard on 15 October. Five days before, he wrote to Durand:

> I've just spent five hours with Chevillard in two days, including a three-hour rehearsal this morning . . . That's a lot of Chevillard for a single man . . . As you can imagine, I'm absolutely shattered. The fellow ought to have been a wild beast tamer. You have to admire the way he makes people work, but otherwise what a Caliban!!!

Not that Debussy can have been the easiest composer to have hovering at rehearsals. Years later the first oboist of the Lamoureux Orchestra, François Gillet, recalled that during one of them Debussy said to Chevillard:

> 'un peu plus vite ici' . . . So Chevillard said: 'Mon cher ami, yesterday you gave me the tempo we have just played.' Debussy looked at him with intense reflection in his eyes and said: 'But I *don't feel music* the *same way every day*.'

As Léon Vallas has pointed out, the critics at that first performance can be divided into two camps: those who felt Debussy had succeeded in producing something quite new, and those who blamed him for not offering them a rewrite of the *Nocturnes* or of the sea music in *Pelléas*. Of the latter camp, no more need be said. From Debussy's supporters, the most accurate and sensible comments were those of M.-D.

Calvocoressi, a friend of Ravel, who wrote in *Le guide musical* a week after the performance:

> *La mer* seems to me to mark a new phase in Debussy's evolution: the inspiration is more masculine (*mâle*), the colours purer and the outlines sharper... One has the impression that M. Debussy, after all the time he spent exploring the possibilities of sound, has here considerably condensed and clarified the mass of his discoveries and his music is on the way to acquiring that absolute rhythmic rightness (*eurythmie*) which is the hallmark of masterpieces...

La mer marked one step forward in Debussy's critical standing in that even those who found the work incoherent or 'unseaworthy' could no longer fall back on the old charges of femininity, lassitude or decadence. Debussy's *eurythmie* took longer to find general acceptance, but more recently investigations by Roy Howat have confirmed that *La mer* is indeed most carefully structured.[11]

Also in that October of 1905, Durand published the first set of Debussy's *Images* which had been occupying the composer since at least the end of 1901. On holiday in Eastbourne, he suddenly discovered that 'the first piece, "Reflets dans l'eau", doesn't satisfy me at all so I decided to write another based on different ideas and in accordance with the most recent discoveries of harmonic chemistry'. Making allowances for the composer's habitual flippancy about his composing methods, we can indeed discern an exploration of piano textures that goes beyond what he had attempted in *Estampes*; and, as in the third piece, 'Mouvement', the logic tends to be circular rather than conventionally forward in its assumptions.

The central 'Hommage à Rameau' was possibly begun after the other two – maybe in 1903, in the wake of the performances of Rameau's opera *Castor et Pollux* and his pastoral ballet *La guirlande*, both conducted by Vincent d'Indy (for two men so often represented as musical opposites, it is surprising how often d'Indy's and Debussy's names are linked!). But, as in the *Trois chansons de France*, historical authenticity was not Debussy's game: his homage to Rameau lies at a deeper level of love and respect for what, in a newspaper article of February 1903, he called Rameau's 'delicate, charming tenderness'. Even the tremendous central climax is the result of what feels like natural, organic growth – Debussy's *eurythmie* once more.

The last, and happiest, event for Debussy of October 1905 was the birth on Monday 30th of a daughter, Claude-Emma, who shared her parents' names on her birth certificate but was always called by her pet name Chouchou. Debussy, not surprisingly, found the experience of becoming a father for the first time at forty-three disturbing, if delightful. We may suppose, though, that broken nights were not part of his routine in the way they might have been today: the presence of nurses and other servants was taken for granted and they barely surface in contemporary accounts of Debussy's life first with Lilly and then with Emma. But a reminiscence from René Peter indicates that they were at times the recipients of disarming candour:

> He was working one morning when his cat began to circle round his legs. At first he paid no attention. The cat miaowed.
>
> 'Yes, yes, you're a lovely cat!' said Claude, stroking her but keeping on with his work.
>
> More miaows.
>
> 'Yes, you are!'
>
> 'Miaow!'
>
> 'Line, you're being a bore!'
>
> Silence. The cat goes back to her cushion and goes to sleep. Claude concentrates on his music. There's a knock.
>
> 'Come in!'
>
> The maid appears to announce lunch; but instead of that she gives a scream.
>
> 'Oh, the dirty animal!'
>
> 'What?' says Claude. 'What's the matter?'
>
> 'Oh!' says Claude as well. 'My carpet!'
>
> The indignant maid makes as if to strike the cat.
>
> 'And if you beat her,' says Claude, suddenly calm, 'will that solve anything? Or do anything for my carpet? The poor animal, she did her best to warn me, and I was the one who didn't respond. She didn't

have her little tray, it's not her fault. What would you do, I wonder, if you'd been shut in without your little tray?'

The maid's cry of 'Oh, monsieur!!!' has to be imagined. But in any conflict between fashionable politeness and reality, Debussy was always likely to choose the latter; likewise in any conflict between humans and animals.

To a biographer, the year 1906 looks to have been an almost empty one in Debussy's life. But playing with Chouchou, worrying about her health or simply watching her no doubt occupied many of his waking hours. He revised the orchestration of two movements from his Prix de Rome cantata *L'enfant prodigue*, wrote 'Serenade for the Doll' which was to become the third movement of *Children's Corner* and was also working on *Ibéria* and on *Le diable dans le beffroi*, while resisting Laloy's attempts in the early months of 1906 to have him revive M. Croche in a series of articles on music:

> Don't you agree, we ought to adopt a more guarded attitude? We need to preserve a little of the 'mystery', which is eventually going to be rendered 'pervious' by all this gossip and tittle-tattle, with the artists joining in like so many aged actresses.

The only article he did write to break a three-year silence, in the magazine *Musica*, was on Charles Gounod in July. What prompted it remains unknown, unless it was the 1,000th performance of *Faust*, given at the Opéra a year earlier – not a really convincing reason. It may simply be that he was coming increasingly to identify with his one-time protector, since three of the qualities he attributes to Gounod were ones he might have wished to apply to himself: those of belonging to no school, of serving as an antidote to Wagner, and of stirring the emotions of a large number of his contemporaries, a task to which 'no one would deny that Gounod gave generously of his time'. The public battles in Paris over Wagner had by now been largely won: the only two of his operas that had still not been staged there by 1906 were *Das Rheingold* and *Parsifal*, although the Opéra did not mount a complete Ring cycle until 1911, conducted by Weingartner. But the private

13 Debussy with his parents in 1906

battles of French composers with 'the ghost of old Klingsor' were very far from over, nor was Debussy immune from its influence. Might this article on Gounod be read to some extent as a bout of whistling in the dark to keep Debussy's spirits up?

His life took on more outward action at the very end of the year with the fourth revival of *Pelléas* at the Opéra-Comique on 23 December, preceded by rehearsals at which Debussy's temper was frayed by the way the opera was turning into a routine exercise, and then with the opera's Brussels premiere on 9 January, its first performance abroad, for which he travelled to the Belgian capital on 27 December.

Understandably, not being versed in the difficulties of life in an opera house and without a Messager or a Carré to help take the strain, Debussy at rehearsals homed in on all the things that went wrong. Anguished letters to Durand and Laloy tell of the bell in Act v that gave a C instead of a G so that 'it sounds rather as if it's dinner time in the castle'; and of how 'the woodwind were thick and noisy, the brass on the other hand were stuffed with cotton wool'; while the dungeons were 'so realistic no one can get into them'.

Debussy did not stay for the premiere on the Wednesday evening but, if we are to believe him, reached Paris only on the Saturday evening, the 12th, thus missing the noisy first performance of Ravel's song cycle *Histoires naturelles*. He had to content himself with a copy of the score sent to him by Durand towards the end of February. It was from this time that various critics, headed by the disputatious Emile Vuillermoz, began to write of Ravel as being Debussy's successor and even as bidding fair to outpace his elder. Laloy sprang to Debussy's defence but the best defence would have been a new work from Debussy himself. Was he written out, as Vuillermoz seemed to imply?

This was a question that Debussy, under his insignia 'toujours plus haut', must often have asked himself during the last ten years of his life, as the weight of past successes began to tell. *Ibéria* and *Le diable* still hung fire. Meanwhile, in May, he was confronted with the past genius of Musorgsky in extracts from *Boris Godunov* in one of Diaghilev's five Russian historical concerts and with the very present genius of Richard Strauss conducting *Salome*: 'I don't see how anyone', he wrote to the impresario Gabriel Astruc, 'can be other than enthusiastic about this work – an absolute masterpiece . . . almost as rare a phenomenon as the appearance of a comet.'

During the summer Debussy toyed with the idea of writing an opera based on Joseph Bédier's *Roman de Tristan* and on 2 August, driven out of the house by a defective boiler, left with his wife and daughter for the Grand Hotel in Pourville, where they stayed until the middle of September. The orchestral *Images* were still causing problems, being, as he told Durand on 5 August, 'well written, but with that skill born of habit (*ce coutumier métier*) that's so hard to conquer and so tiresome'. Just as *Pelléas* at the Opéra-Comique was settling into a rut, so there was the ever-present danger of the same happening to what Debussy called his 'thinking machine'. Musorgsky, Wagner, Strauss, Ravel, the Debussystes . . . the machine was having a lot to cope with at this time.

Nonetheless, in October it began to turn over once again. True, Debussy had to explain to his one-time colleague Gabriel Pierné that, no, he could not play the central movement of *La mer* on its own (shades of d'Indy and the *Fantaisie*, or 'how to be misunderstood by those who should know better'), but he did have the pleasure of getting to know the twenty-eight-year-old composer, timpanist and conductor André Caplet, who had beaten Ravel to win the Prix de Rome in 1901. Caplet was to be a tower of strength for Debussy in the years up to the First World War, not least as 'the graveyard of errors' when overseeing proofs of his music.

Debussy's answer to any critics who thought he was over the hill also appeared that October, in the form of the second book of piano *Images* – again a triptych: one of over twenty such groupings to be found between the *Trois mélodies* of 1891 and the three-movement Violin Sonata finished in 1917. The 'threeness' here extends to the layout of the piano writing, now on three staves. He had already experimented with this in 'La soirée dans Grenade' and in *D'un cahier d'esquisses*, a piece written around 1903 which may, either in its present or in a somewhat different form, have been intended at one time as the central panel in another triptych, flanked by *Masques* and *L'isle joyeuse*.[12] Perhaps we should not make too much of the triple layout: writing on three staves can be found in some late-nineteenth-century piano transcriptions, such as Chabrier's of his own *Habanera*. But the fact that Debussy's first *Image*, 'Cloches à travers les feuilles', enters the same world as Ravel's 'La vallée des cloches' from *Miroirs* (and the only one of those five pieces to employ three staves) does suggest that the older composer was squaring up to his younger rival.

The second panel of the triptych, 'Et la lune descend sur le temple qui fut' (And the moon goes down behind the ruined temple), leads on from 'Pagodes' in its exploitation, not so much of Oriental sounds like the gamelan, as of an Oriental stillness and stasis. The first chord belongs, in the Western tradition, as part of a cadence in sixteenth-century religious music, achieved through strict part-writing; Debussy gives it a quite new feeling by treating it as a non-cadential chord with no sense of part-writing whatever. As in his remark to his maid, context is crucial to meaning and impact.

Finally 'Poissons d'or' charts the imagined swoops and twitches of two large carp as featured on a Japanese plaque in black lacquer, touched up with mother-of-pearl and gold, which hung on the wall of the composer's study. It is the only piece of his which relates directly to the Oriental *objets d'art* on which he spent such large amounts of money; amounts which, in all probability, have been far superseded by royalties from this delightfully playful portrait of piscine life.

It must have been around that October that plans began to hatch in London to bring Debussy over to conduct some of his orchestral works. Henry Wood went to Paris to negotiate a fee and, after Debussy had turned down 100 guineas, offered him 200, which was accepted (throughout this pre-war period the exchange rate was around 25 francs to the pound – 5,250 francs represented more than twice Debussy's income from royalties in 1905). So began the series of conducting and playing engagements which was to take him to seven foreign countries over the next six years, reinforcing his view that idolatry and victimization were, on a number of fronts, barely distinguishable from one another.

6 Travels and travails (1908–1914)

Debussy's preparations for conducting at the Queen's Hall in London on 1 February were musical and, possibly, personal as well. On two successive Sundays, 19 and 26 January, he conducted *La mer* with the Colonne Orchestra. He wrote to Segalen on 15 January:

> It was not without a furiously beating heart I climbed the rostrum yesterday morning for the first rehearsal. It's the first time in my life I've tried my hand at orchestral conducting and certainly I bring to the task a candid inexperience which ought to disarm those curious beasts called 'orchestral musicians'. At least, they're full of goodwill.
>
> Further impressions: you really feel yourself to be the heart of your own music . . . When it 'sounds' properly, you seem yourself to have become an instrument embracing all possible sonorities, unleashed merely by waving a tiny stick.

For all his trepidation, some of those who had heard the first performance of *La mer* under Chevillard felt they were now really hearing the work for the first time.

In between these two performances, on 20 January, Debussy and Emma got married. We cannot know for certain why they chose this moment to regularize their relationship, but it is at least possible that his forthcoming high-profile visit to London with Emma lay behind the move.

At the Queen's Hall on 1 February a crowded audience gave him what Henry Wood called 'a real English welcome'. Both *L'après-midi*

and La mer went well, although the anonymous critic of The Times was
not wholly converted to the Debussy camp: readers were informed on
3 February that 'as in all his maturer works, it is obvious that he
renounces melody as definitely as Alberich renounces love' and that
'for perfect enjoyment of this music there is no attitude of mind more
to be recommended than the passive, unintelligent rumination of the
typical amateur of the mid-Victorian era'. But Debussy was now a
firmly entered figure on the British musical map and it should remain
a matter of some pride for that nation that the first two biographies of
the composer appeared in London and Edinburgh in 1908 – by Louise
Liebich and W. H. Daly respectively.

Back in Paris, Debussy heard Viñes give the first performance of the
second book of Images on 21 February, to an almost totally unre-
sponsive audience, but otherwise, as he told Durand a few weeks later,
'as for the "whirlwind that is Paris", permit me to keep my distance!'
Increasingly from now on, Debussy became reclusive, making occasional forays into the outside world to conduct or play for much-
needed money, and even at home he never entertained on a large scale.
As his debts to his publishers and others mounted, he concentrated
ever more intensely on the operatic projects that might not only relieve
his money worries but also signal an advance on Pelléas. The performances of that opera in June 1908, with Maggie Teyte as Mélisande,
did not please him; as for his original Pelléas, Debussy told Durand
'one rather amusing detail is that everyone says Périer is getting better
and better . . . The reason, I'm sure, is that he's entirely given up
singing what I wrote.' It says much for the composer's idealism (or
impecuniousness?) that, despite these proofs of the fallibility of opera
singers, he persevered with work on Orphée with Segalen, on Tristan
with Mourey and, in solitude, on The Devil in the Belfry and on another
Poe tale, The Fall of the House of Usher. None was finished at the time of
his death.

Perhaps as a counterbalance to these ideas projected into an
indefinite future, he turned also to the past: to re-orchestrating his
cantata L'enfant prodigue, and to writing Trois chansons for unaccompa-

14 Chouchou

nied choir on poems by Charles d'Orléans. These were a far cry from the 'atmospheric' writing attributed to him so widely by British critics, recalling as they do the *chansons* of the sixteenth century in their clear textures and rhythms. The first one is a revision of a setting from 1898, but the last two were new. Although he had set the third song, 'Yver, vous n'estes qu'un villain', in 1898, the published version is very different, with conventional imitative entries that occur nowhere else in Debussy's *œuvre*: might this have been an ironic comment to the effect that such a blatant technical formula was, like winter, 'villain'?

A precisely analogous use of formula opens the piano suite *Children's Corner*, finished in July and dedicated 'to my dear little Chouchou, with her father's tender apologies for what follows'. 'Doctor Gradus ad Parnassum' looks forward to a time when Chouchou will be practising her piano exercises – a plain projection of a father's hopes on to a daughter who, from her earliest years, looked more like him than like her mother (in 1911 Stravinsky noticed that 'her teeth were exactly like her father's, i.e. like tusks').[1] The other five movements are free of hopes and merely celebrate the life that is, whether real (her doll, her toy elephant, Jimbo, and her golliwog) or imaginary (the dancing snow, the little shepherd). In the event, no apologies were needed for this delightful music which Debussy entrusted to the American pianist Harold Bauer. Of that first performance on 23 December, and of the 'Golliwogg's Cake Walk' in particular with its parody of the first bars of *Tristan and Isolde*, Bauer later wrote:

> The hall was full. To my chagrin, Debussy was not there. I played the suite and went out into the courtyard of the old house whose ballroom had been converted into an auditorium. I found the composer walking up and down with a very sour face. He came up to me and said, 'Eh bien! How did they take it?'
>
> I was immediately filled with an immense pity for him. I realized that this great man, who had struggled so long to obtain recognition of the new idiom he was bringing to our art, was *nervous*, scared to death at the thought that his reputation might be compromised because he had written something humorous. I looked him straight in the eye. 'They laughed', I said briefly. I saw relief pour through him. He burst into a stentorian roar of glee and shook me warmly by the hand.

This wave of enthusiasm carried over into the New Year. After completing the full score of 'Ibéria' on Christmas Day he went on to finish the short scores of its two companions: 'Rondes de printemps' on 30 December and 'Gigues' on 4 January. As if in recognition of the stature of these works, at the beginning of February Fauré invited Debussy to join the Conseil supérieur, the governing body, of the Conservatoire. Debussy was happy to accept, not only for the honour itself and the chance of having an official voice in the future of French music, but perhaps also for the pledge it represented of Fauré's personal support – and of his acceptance that their dual relationship with Emma Bardac need not stand between them. The appointment caused a furore in the musical Establishment, in line with other changes in the institution which had gained Fauré the nickname 'Robespierre'.

At the end of February Debussy returned to London to conduct *L'après-midi* and the *Nocturnes* with the Queen's Hall Orchestra, which

had again been rehearsed by Henry Wood. The audience was delighted when he got lost in 'Fêtes' and tried unsuccessfully to stop the
orchestra. An encore was demanded and, wrote Wood, 'this time
nothing went wrong and the ovation was even greater than before.
Debussy was nonplussed and certainly did not understand the
English mind'. The cult of the 'gallant amateur' has never really
crossed the Channel . . .

After the concert on 27 February Debussy and Emma had to attend
a reception organized by the 'Music Club' in the Aeolian Hall. 'What
figure shall I cut there?' he wrote back to Durand late that afternoon.
The answer comes from the young Arnold Bax, who remembered that
the president of the Club, Alfred Kalisch, made a speech in something
that might have been French:

> The great composer, an inordinately shy man, was planted in a chair
> in the exact centre of the platform facing the audience. He was clearly
> utterly nonplussed, and could only attempt to solve his problem by
> rising and making a stiff little bow whenever he recognized his own
> name amid Kalisch's guttural mumblings.
>
> This part of the ordeal over, he was permitted to shamble dazedly
> to the rear of the hall, where he confided to Edwin Evans that he
> would rather write a symphony to order than go through such an
> experience again.

The truth was that, linguistic problems aside, Debussy was ill.
Visits to Edinburgh and Manchester were cancelled and on his return
home he complained of almost daily haemorrhages. The evidence
suggests that these, possibly linked with haemorrhoids, may have
been the first signs of the rectal cancer which was to kill him nine
years later.

But in May, after completing the orchestration of 'Rondes de printemps' on the 10th, he was back in London for the rehearsals and the
British premiere of *Pelléas* at Covent Garden. As in Brussels, rehearsals
did not find the composer at his most patient: his most vigorous complaints were of the producer who, as he confided in Durand, 'comes
from Marseilles, sees platforms where there's nothing but empty

space and imagines wonderful flowering bushes on struts as naked as a blind man's stick . . . I've rarely had such a strong desire to kill anybody'. In general the opera was well received; those critics who did not fully understand it were by now moved to be cautious and ask for further exposure to the work before pontificating.

In July he accepted a further invitation from Fauré and sat on the jury for the woodwind *concours* at the Conservatoire, where he was impressed by the high standard of the flutes, oboes and clarinets; 'as for the bassoons, they're admirable . . . the sound of the instrument is tending towards pathos and, mark my words, that's going to alter certain orchestral "values"' – a comment strangely prophetic of the opening of *Le sacre du printemps*. He was less impressed, though, with the bassoon test piece, a *Fantaisie* by Henri Busser 'written', as he decribed it to Caplet, 'as if he'd been born inside a bassoon . . . – which is not to say he was born to make music'. Significantly, Debussy was happy for Busser to apply his workmanlike technical skills on orchestrating the *Petite suite* in 1907 and again on *Printemps* in 1912.

At the beginning of September Louis Laloy published the first French biography of Debussy for which he had had the benefit of conversations with the composer, but which, as François Lesure points out, contains several remarks that sound far from 'authentic'.[2] But Debussy was doubtless far more irritated by the article of a M. Raphaël Cor which appeared in October, entitled 'M. Claude Debussy et le snobisme contemporain'. Debussy's music 'claimed to eschew any element of melody', it promoted 'states of vague reverie' linking it with opium and morphine, and there was

> one merit which one could not refuse M. Debussy; that of having had a nice instinct for the subjects that really suit him. He needs heroes who are pale-complexioned, delicate, always on the languid side. Rossetti, Mallarmé and Maeterlinck were well chosen to inspire him. On the other hand, when he decided to tackle Baudelaire, he could only diminish his poetry and make it peculiarly insipid.[3]

The editors of the journal in which the article appeared then improved the shining hour by sending out a questionnaire to various journalists and musicians, asking them what was Debussy's importance, what role he should play in the evolution of contemporary music and whether he should become the head of a school of composers. Needless to say, at the end of this exercise the water was, if anything, muddier than before. But Debussy would certainly have identified with Reynaldo Hahn's claim that 'if I have a high opinion of Debussy, I am not a Debussyste and I regard the Debussystes as unfortunates'.

Debussy must have expressed to Fauré his admiration of the wind teaching at the Conservatoire because the latter now commissioned him to write the clarinet test piece for the 1910 *concours*. At the same time Debussy began writing the first book of *Préludes*, which he completed with 'La danse de Puck' on 4 February. Was he perhaps encouraged to write for piano by serving on the jury for the Conservatoire entrance examinations in November? He wrote to Caplet on 25 November:

> I've been dedicating myself to the betterment of the pianistic race in France . . . Life's habitual irony saw to it that the most artistic of all the candidates was a young Brazilian girl of thirteen. She's not beautiful, but her eyes are 'drunk with music' and she has that ability to cut herself off from her surroundings which is the rare but characteristic mark of the artist.

The young girl in question was Guiomar Novaes, who went on to have an international career.

Debussy too must have cut himself off from Emma and Chouchou for most of that Christmas ('Les collines d'Anacapri' dates from Boxing Day and 'Des pas sur la neige' from the day after), and work on the clarinet *Rapsodie* and further *Préludes* continued through January, in the final weeks of which the Seine rose from its usual depth of 7 feet to over 20 feet, flooding large areas of the city. Unfortunately, 'La cathédrale engloutie' is one of the three *Préludes* that are not dated . . .

On 20 February 1910 *Ibéria* was given its first performance, conducted by Gabriel Pierné. If, some twenty years earlier, Debussy had regarded Pierné's rise through the musical Establishment with some awe, he now had to work hard to create some sympathy between Ibéria's essence and Pierné's conducting. He reported to Caplet on the first performance and then on the rehearsal for the second on 27 February:

> only the third movement worked as it should . . . The ultra-Spanish rhythm of the first went all 'Left-Bank' under our young Capellmeister's intelligent conducting and the 'perfumes of the night' seeped out discreetly from under a bolster, presumably so as not to upset anybody . . .
>
> This morning, rehearsal of Ibéria . . . it's going better. The aforementioned young Capellmeister and his orchestra have consented to be less earthbound and to take wing somewhat . . . You can't imagine how naturally the transition works between 'Parfums de la nuit' and 'Le matin d'un jour de fête'. It sounds as though it's improvised.

. . . and that effect of improvisation marked the ultimate goal in Debussy's attempt to get away from the constraints of an orthodox, learned technique – the sort of technique that governs Pierné's own music and prevents it, by and large, from 'taking wing'.

By 1910 the Franck faction, led by Vincent d'Indy, had acquired a firm grip of the Société nationale and increasingly it was becoming difficult for composers who did not subscribe to the Franckian aesthetic to get a hearing there. In response to this situation Ravel and a number of other Fauré pupils founded an alternative Sociéte musicale indépendante, and on 20 April an inaugural concert of first performances was given in the Salle Gaveau, including works by Fauré, Ravel and Debussy: Fauré was the accompanist in his song cycle La chanson d'Eve, two young girls of six and ten played Ma mère l'oye and Ravel performed Debussy's D'un cahier d'esquisses. We do not know whether Debussy was present, but he showed his sympathy for the new society by playing four of his Préludes for the first time in public at its fourth concert on 25 May; the last of the group, 'La danse de Puck', was encored. It is worth noting that, presumably at his request, a rather ancient salon-sized Erard was hired for the occasion. 'No one

15 Arthur Rackham: 'The fairies are exquisite dancers' (J. M. Barrie, *Peter Pan in Kensington Gardens*)

can imagine,' wrote one listener, 'the gentleness of his caressing style, the subtlety of his singing touch which said so much, as it were in a whisper . . .'⁴ As the pianist Robert Schmitz later recalled:

> Crescendos in those days were one of Debussy's obsessions in piano playing. He liked slight crescendos, a ppp increasing into a mere pp . . . Another thing Debussy insisted upon was the proper way to strike a note on the piano. 'It must be struck in a peculiar way', he would say, 'otherwise the sympathetic vibrations of the other notes will not be heard quivering distantly in the air.' Debussy regarded the piano as the Balinese musicians regard their gamelan orchestras.

It is not surprising then that when Debussy played the piano abroad, on pianos and in halls he did not know, there were sometimes complaints that he was practically inaudible.

The months of May, June and July were unusually busy ones for him. For six years he had written no songs – by some way the longest song-free period in his composing career. Now, in what might seem a rather self-conscious attempt at self-renewal, he went back again to the seventeenth-century poet Tristan Lhermite and beyond that to the fifteenth century poet and vagabond François Villon, one of the earliest *marginaux* in French literary history. Interestingly, whereas his renewed acquaintance with Lhermite produces a substyle that might loosely be called 'neo-Renaissance', in the first two of the Villon songs the quasi-modal inflections are intimately bound in with chromatic, unmistakably twentieth-century harmonic and rhythmic gestures. It is as if Debussy felt empathy for Villon's marginal lifestyle – even envy of its freedom, since we know that his marriage was going through a particularly difficult period, with Emma writing to a lawyer about a possible separation.[5]

After attending the premiere of Stravinsky's *The Firebird* on 25 June (when asked by Stravinsky a few years later for his real feelings about the work, he replied 'Oh well, you had to start somewhere . . .'), he was again delighted with the winning performance at the Conservatoire clarinet *concours* of his own *Rapsodie* and of the *Petite pièce* he had provided as a sightreading test. He was also glad (perhaps, given his habitual insecurity, even delighted) to be able to tell Durand that 'to judge by the expressions on the faces of my colleagues, the *Rapsodie* was a success!'

But despite this success and that of the *Préludes* (only three weeks after their publication on 14 April Ravel was enthusing over them as 'wonderful masterpieces')[6] Debussy was desperately worried over money. This must have played a large part in his acceptance of a contract on 30 September to write a ballet called *Isis* for the Canadian dancer Maud Allan. By far the best part of the deal was that it brought him 10,000 francs on signature.

On 28 October his father died. This came, as he wrote to Caplet, 'after a long and painful illness. Even though we hardly ever agreed about anything, it's a loss I feel more deeply with every day that passes . . . I'm getting ready to leave for Vienna and Budapest in several days' time. I'm playing the orchestra in the first and the piano in the second. To say that my delight is unalloyed would be to tell a lie.'

Needless to say, money was again the spur. By means of an interpreter and elaborate pantomime gestures he achieved reasonable performances of the *Petite Suite* and *L'après-midi* and a vivid one of 'Ibéria', but both *La mer* and the *Nocturnes* had to be abandoned. There were clearly recidivist elements in the Konzertverein Orchestra, since he wrote to Emma on 2 December: 'I don't think a man playing the viola should consider he has the right not to play – what a nonsense! – and gaze at me as though I were a shop-window!' Nor was he pleased to be congratulated in the course of a toast at dinner with having abolished melody (perhaps the speaker had been reading Raphaël Cor's article in *Le cas Debussy*); to which he responded sharply that 'all my music aspires to be nothing but melody'.[7]

He was happier in Budapest, where he stayed from 3 to 6 December and where he had no orchestra to deal with. Instead he played the *Estampes* and *Children's Corner* and accompanied the soprano Rose Féart in the *Proses lyriques* – this despite his comment to Durand when she had sung Mélisande in London in May of the previous year that she was 'indescribably ugly and lacking in poetry . . . Naturally, she sings the notes, but there's nothing behind them.' Such were the demands of his impoverished condition. His happiest moments were spent listening to the gypsy fiddler Radics, whose name appeared at least three times in the composer's letters over the coming months. Here was the counterbalance to Vienna, 'an old city covered in make-up, over-stuffed with the music of Brahms and Puccini, the officers with chests like women and the women with chests like officers'. Radics, by contrast, as he told Robert Godet,

> in an unpretentious, run-of-the-mill café . . . gives the impression of sitting in the shade of a forest and, from the depths of men's souls, seeks out that peculiar melancholy we so rarely have the chance to make use of. He could extract confidences from a safe.

In the circumstances, Vienna was a fitting place for him to receive a letter from the Italian poet and playwright Gabriele d'Annunzio, asking him to write incidental music for his French verse-play *Le martyre de Saint Sébastien*. Androgynous officers were nothing compared with the inspiration behind *Le martyre*. D'Annunzio had been fascinated by the love-bites left on his chest by his mistress Olga Ossani. They looked like fresh arrow wounds and, for the first time, the image of Saint Sebastian pierced with arrows rose up before his eyes.[8]

Back in Paris, Debussy spent the period over the New Year working on the ballet *Isis*, now renamed *Khamma*, and perhaps on some of the second book of *Préludes*. But from 11 January 1911, when Act III of *Le martyre* finally reached him, almost up to the premiere at the Châtelet theatre on 22 May, Debussy was fully engaged on d'Annunzio's text. As Robert Orledge has pointed out, *Le martyre* contains 'about 55 minutes of music in its original stage version, nearly three times as much as any of his ballets'.[9] Debussy may have been indulging in his habitual exaggeration when he claimed in an interview of the time to have written 'in two months a score that would normally take me a year', but it was hard labour for him nonetheless.

In the early stages at least, he was ambivalent about the whole project, as was Emma. It seems d'Annunzio had been clever enough to engage her sympathies in December 1910, but on a piano reduction of the score Debussy wrote, in June 1911: 'For my own little one, in memory of three months [sic] of Martyrdom which she alone knew how to alleviate with the happy phrase: "What does a work like this matter to you!"' Debussy himself wrote to Robert Godet on 6 February in an uncertain vein:

> I need hardly tell you that in it the cult of Adonis mingles with that of Jesus; that it is very fine, beyond a doubt [*très beau, par affirmation*]; and that, in fact, if I'm allowed enough time, there are some opportunities for good music.

Whether Debussy realized those opportunities has been a matter of debate ever since. He himself was moved to tears of emotion when he heard his music performed and it has always had to fight a difficult battle against d'Annunzio's very long and over-perfumed text. And yet shorn of this entirely, as in the four-movement suite made by Caplet, the music does sound incomplete. Without question, the project marked a new departure for Debussy on the spiritual front, going some way beyond the pale pre-Raphaelitism of *La damoiselle élue*. There is a story that during the long arguments over the representation of Paradise in Act v, the designer Bakst said to Debussy: 'You've been to Paradise then, have you?' To which the composer replied: 'Yes, but I never discuss it with strangers.' Behind this *bon mot*, what a store of disillusionment! First *Pelléas*; now *Le martyre*; would *Usher* and *The Devil* fare any better?

Three days before the premiere of *Le martyre*, another premiere had taken place, at the Opéra-Comique, of Ravel's one-act comic opera *L'heure espagnole*. We do not know whether Debussy went to see it, but it would be hard to imagine anything more different from *Le martyre*. Whether as a result of this or not, press speculation over Debussy's influence on Ravel or vice versa now abated significantly.

Partly this may have been due to a new star appearing on the musical horizon. While the Opéra declared its final acceptance of Wagner from 10 to 14 June with its first production of the complete *Ring*, conducted by Weingartner, at the Châtelet on 13 June Diaghilev's Ballets Russes gave the premiere of Stravinsky's *Petrushka*. This was the only one of Stravinsky's three pre-war ballets about which Debussy had no reservations, and the influence of its brittle, brash sound-world can be felt in many of Debussy's later works. He told Stravinsky some months later:

> There's a sort of sonorous magic about it, mysteriously transforming these mechanical souls into human beings: it's a spell which, so far, I think you are alone in possessing. And then there are orchestral *certainties* such as I have encountered only in *Parsifal* – I'm sure you'll understand what I mean!

Five years later, he was still enthusiastic, writing on 26 May 1917 to Diaghilev that '*Petrushka* is definitely a masterpiece. They haven't anything of the sort in Germany and never will have.' It is also clear from these two comments that he regarded *Parsifal* as the end of the line for German music.

On 19 June Debussy, Emma and Chouchou left for Turin where Debussy was to rehearse and conduct L'après-midi and 'Ibéria'. Although he did not let on about the fact to Durand, to whom he complained that 'six hours of rehearsal a day are enough to give you a distaste for any sort of music, your own included', in fact, after a few desperate minutes of rehearsal during which he insisted on turning over pages of the score with the hand holding the baton, he made way for the young Vittorio Gui and reappeared on the rostrum only for the concert itself. Even then, according to Gui, he conducted 'woodenly, mechanically, without fire and without really leading his forces; no calamities, but no poetic feeling'.

Not surprisingly, on his return to Paris at the end of June Debussy was ordered by his doctor to take a month's rest. A holiday was postponed because Emma's daughter Dolly de Tinan was about to give birth, but the family then spent the whole of August at Houlgate, on the Channel coast just to the west of Pourville. Even here Debussy worked. He wrote to Caplet on the 15th that 'the firm of Durfils [Durand et Fils], who are not in the business of marketing leisure, have sent me the proofs of the orchestral score of Le martyre de Saint Sébastien'. He was also busy orchestrating the clarinet Rapsodie.

The last four months of the year were months of depression, largely brought on by Emma's refusal to let him go to Boston to see a production of Pelléas conducted by Caplet. He managed to finish the piano scores of 'Gigues' and Khamma by January, but little else. As to the two Poe operas, the situation remained as it had been the year before, when he told a New York Times interviewer:

> I can't force myself. It's just like producing vegetables or anything else. If you put a lot of chemicals and goodness knows what in the earth you may be able to raise salad in winter, but it is not the real, true salad and doesn't taste like it. And in the same way music born under such conditions is not true music – it is a hot-house product.[10]

In these difficult months Debussy was obviously much concerned with the way his brain was, or was not, functioning and with the path his music might take from here on. Two letters he wrote in December

16 Debussy and André Caplet, c. 1910

tell of this with unusual eloquence. First, on 18 December, to Robert Godet:

> The longer I go on, the more I detest the sort of intentional disorder whose aim is merely to deceive the ear. The same goes for bizarre,

intriguing harmonies which are no more than parlour-games . . . How much has first to be discovered, then suppressed, before one can reach the naked flesh of emotion . . . pure instinct ought to warn us, anyway, that textures and colours are no more than illusory disguises!

Four days later, he confided to Caplet:

I can't finish the two Poe stories, everything is as dull as a hole in the ground. For every bar that has some freedom about it, there are twenty that are stifled by the weight of one particular tradition; try as I may, I'm forced to recognize its hypocritical and destructive influence. The fact that this tradition belongs to me by right is hardly relevant . . . it's just as depressing, because whatever masks you wear, underneath you find yourself.

From this it seems as though Debussy was obsessed by two ideas: that the 'musique à moi' he had been seeking for twenty years and more was still liable to be obfuscated by learned techniques; and that, even when he was able to shed those techniques, the music which was left was not worth having. Altogether his depression is easy to understand.

The year 1912 was relatively quiet for him, if one judges merely by external events. There were no journeys and he occupied himself orchestrating *Khamma* and 'Gigues', finishing the second book of *Préludes* and, in August and September, composing the ballet *Jeux*. But the year contained at least four events, ranging from the public to the intimate, calculated to disturb the best-balanced of psyches.

The first, and by some way the most public, was the premiere on 29 May of Nijinsky's ballet based on *L'après-midi d'un faune*. In Nijinsky's choreography, the ballet ends with the Faun picking up a veil dropped by the Nymphs; he

holds up the veil, nuzzles in it, then stretching it out on the ground, lowers himself on it, head tucked under, and finally, as muted horns and harp harmonics over a quiet flute chord conclude the choreographic poem, consummates his union with it, taut on the ground, by a convulsive jerk.[11]

The result was one of the scandals for which Paris has been notorious and at the second performance the police were present. Debussy wisely kept silent about the final gesture, but we may guess that such an extravert display of sexuality, so far removed from the emotional implicitness at the heart of the score and of the whole Symbolist movement that gave birth to it, cannot but have offended him. Certainly he resented the discrepancy between the supple music and the angular choreography – what he termed 'an atrocious "dissonance" with no possible resolution', though only in the decent obscurity of an interview with an Italian journalist in Rome in 1914.[12]

The second disturbing event, if our understanding of the chronology is correct, took place on 9 June when Debussy played the bass and Stravinsky the treble in a piano duet rendering of *Le Sacre du printemps*; or at least of some of it, since, according to Eric Walter White, Stravinsky 'continued working on the score when he returned to Ustilug and Clarens after visiting Paris and London in the summer of 1912, and the "Sacrificial Dance" was completed on 17 November'[13] – after which Stravinsky still had to write the Introduction to Part Two. Laloy, in whose house the playthrough took place, recalled: 'we were dumbfounded, overwhelmed by this hurricane which had come from the depths of the ages and taken our life by the roots'. Note the words 'we' and 'our'. Debussy was not easily dumbfounded by things musical. Well might he, in a letter to the composer of 5 November, refer to that performance as haunting him 'like a beautiful nightmare': from that day on, he had in his mind the terrifying premonition of a musical world that might be not only *post* Debussy but *sine* Debussy.

In between attending performances of Strauss's *Salome* and of *Tristan* on 13 and 20 June, he signed a contract with Diaghilev on the 18th to write the ballet which eventually was given the title *Jeux*. A total fee of 10,000 francs may well have accelerated work on this. In any case, the short score was finished by 25 August, three days after the composer's fiftieth birthday.

Money problems meant that there was no holiday for the Debussy family that summer. Instead, he went on with the difficult task of getting the orchestration of 'Gigues' exactly as he wanted it, with the composition of the second book of *Préludes*, and (the third of the four untoward events) with combating the whims of Maud Allan, who now wanted *Khamma* to be scored for a smaller orchestra and showed the sort of determination that Debussy was used to finding in his wife and his creditors but not among people who commissioned music from him. He complained to Durand on 2 July that

> what she has in mind is not merely an arrangement of my music but a complete rewriting of it by one of those musicians of genius that only England can produce . . . What right has she got to decide that nothing can be done with *Khamma* when she doesn't know the resources it uses and hasn't tried to stage it?

With Charles Koechlin's help, a full score was finally achieved but Maud Allan in 1916 was still complaining that the orchestra needed to be smaller. The first concert performance did not take place until 1924, six years after Debussy's death. For him, then, it came to represent merely a great deal of wasted effort, time and temper.

In November he returned to the trade of music critic, writing eleven articles for the review *SIM* (Société internationale de musique) between then and March 1914, for a fee of 500 francs each. By now, he was confident enough to dispense with his *alter ego* Monsieur Croche when making his more contentious statements: for example, when noting in his December review the jeers meted out by some of the noisier members of the audience to a work that failed to please them:

> M. Théodore Dubois has had the whimsical notion, towards the end of a busy life, of writing a symphony which the audience (in the gallery) emphatically gave him to understand was not a useful addition either to the renown of music in general or to that of French music in particular . . . In art, there can be no obligatory respect and it is by mistakes of this kind that we encumber the path of a host of people who have become respectable only through age. For a long time now we have been subject to a mania for administering things which are essentially non-administrable and, inevitably, this mania has ended up by invading art!

By now, these cries of 'liberté' had become somewhat formulaic and he persisted in ignoring the fact that he himself had been very highly trained. No interviewer, it should be said, ever succeeded in getting him to agree that he would have been a better composer had he never entered the Conservatoire...

Fate reserved her sharpest blow of the year for the very end. On 27 December *Pelléas et Mélisande* reached its 100th performance at the Opéra-Comique. Even though Marguerite Carré, Jean Périer and M. Boulogne (the Mélisande, Pelléas and Golaud respectively) all suffered the lash in Debussy's letters, it was nonetheless an important event and when, at the dinner held to mark the occasion, the Under-Secretary of State for the Arts got up to make a speech, Debussy's promotion from Chevalier to Officier of the Légion d'honneur seemed to be impending. Instead, the rosettes went to d'Indy and to the light opera composer Charles Lecocq.[14] It would be hard to envisage a more deliberate and hurtful snub.

For those members of the public who regarded Debussy, and indeed composers in general, as purveyors who could be expected to produce a steady supply of material, the year 1912 had been disappointing, with no new Debussy works being performed. To some extent this shameful lacuna was addressed in 1913 with four works of very varying size and impact.

On 26 January the composer conducted the Colonne Orchestra in the first complete performance of the *Images*, 'Gigues' having now finally reached its definitive state. Not all the critics had yet caught up with Debussy, and Ravel, in the first of two useful interventions this year, seized the opportunity to lambast the laggards.[15] March saw Debussy giving a preview on the 5th of the first three *Préludes* from the second book (young girls threw flowers at him, which may have assuaged his chagrin over the Légion d'honneur) and on the 31st attending the opening, amid high hopes all round, of the new Théâtre des Champs-Elysées.

On 19 April the second book of *Préludes* was published. One critic had already noted, at the performance cited above, that the first piece of the set, 'Bruyères', contains nothing at all; the second, 'Feuilles mortes', not much more; the third, 'La puerta del vino', though better than the previous two, is nothing out of the ordinary . . . M. Debussy is, of course, a man of talent and a very capable pianist, but can he himself believe that these little sparks deserve the same ovations as masterpieces by Gluck, Beethoven or Mozart?[16]

The first two of those names suggest that the critic in question knew how to wound. It is undoubtedly true that this second book has never achieved the popularity of the first and, despite its nods in the direction of Britain through Arthur Rackham ('Les fées sont d'exquises danseuses' and 'Feuilles mortes') and Dickens ('M. Pickwick'), was greeted on this side of the Channel with some disappointment.[17] This may have been due in part to its greater harmonic complexity, including several reminiscences of *Petrushka*, the score of which Debussy had been studying over the Easter of 1912.

In May 1913 Debussy's 'thinking machine' received two further important jolts. Among the visitors to his house on the avenue du Bois de Boulogne was the *sufi* musician Inayat Khan who, with his cousin and two brothers, made a number of tours in Europe and America. According to the younger brother, Debussy heard them play and then reciprocated with three piano pieces depicting 'the rainy season', 'spring' and 'autumn'. Which these were remains unknown but, as Roy Howat has indicated, it would be hard to get closer to the Indian and *sufi* philosophy of music than the wonderful sentence Debussy included in his SIM article of November 1913, which deserves quotation in the original French:

> seuls, les musiciens ont le privilège de capter toute la poésie de la nuit et du jour, de la terre et du ciel, d'en reconstituer l'atmosphère et d'en rythmer l'immense palpitation.

. . . of which a, necessarily inadequate, English translation might run:

> composers alone have the privilege of capturing all the poetry of night and day, of earth and sky, of recreating their atmosphere and of setting their mighty pulsations within a rhythmic framework.[18]

17 Debussy's autograph of the prelude 'Ce qu'a vu le vent d'ouest'
(Pierpont Morgan Library)

Although Debussy had already finished his ballet *Jeux* by the time he met Inayat Khan, it is tempting to see the work as exemplifying this preoccupation with atmosphere and rhythm, at the expense of more traditional materials such as long tunes and self-proclaiming development sections. The premiere at the Théâtre des Champs-Elysées on 15 May was greeted with reserve. Amid some critical praise, Debussy's music was accused of being no more than an amalgam of chords and orchestral timbres and Nijinsky's choreography, as in *L'après-midi* the year before, of having nothing to do with the music. Debussy too found the choreography to be one of what Arkel in *Pelléas* described as 'meaningless events' and so presumably did Diaghilev, since he never revived the ballet in the sixteen years of life left to him.

By now Debussy was probably becoming inured to theatrical imperfection. But further food for thought came in the shape of *Le sacre du printemps*, premiered a fortnight later on 29 May – a date chosen by the superstitious Diaghilev to coincide with the first anniversary of Nijinsky's *L'après-midi*. Despite Debussy's foreknowledge of *Le sacre*, he could not remain impervious to the impact of the orchestral score in the theatre: it was, he wrote to Caplet that same evening, 'extraordinarily wild . . . As you might say, it's primitive with all modern conveniences!' If he was disposed to take his own advice about the inadmissibility of respect in art, then he may well have savoured, if with some trepidation, Stravinsky's masterly expression of disrespect in *Le sacre*. But extraordinary wildness was not in Debussy's nature. The nearest he ever came to the brutality of *Le sacre* was in the prelude 'Ce qu'a vu le vent d'ouest', now well in the past. If Stravinsky in a general sense encouraged Debussy to look 'toujours plus haut', *Petrushka* seems to have marked the term of his specific influence.

During that summer Debussy worked on two projects whose utter dissimilarity suggests that one may have been a kind of counterbalance to the other (nearly twenty years later, Ravel's work on his two piano concertos was to provide a parallel instance). A new edition had been published earlier in the year of Mallarmé's complete works. Although Debussy seems to have toyed with the idea of making another setting of the poem 'Apparition', presumably to replace his 1884 setting which had not been published, in the end he chose three other poems for his final exercise in a vocal substyle.

The project was not without its practical problems. First, Mallarmé's heirs initially refused Debussy permission to set any of his poems and relented only when Ravel pleaded his cause; and then Debussy discovered the nature of the difficulty – that Ravel had already, in April and May, set two of the same poems as himself, for which the heirs had given him exclusive permission. Having just succeeded in extricating himself from a Debussy v. Ravel contest, he was mortified to find himself thus engaged again. Ravel, perhaps more wisely, just thought the whole thing was rather funny.

In any case, the music of the two settings has little in common. Ravel in 1913 was taken with Stravinsky's *Three Japanese Lyrics*, themselves written under the influence of *Pierrot Lunaire*. Debussy's *Trois poèmes de Stéphane Mallarmé* still have some roots in the substyles of the *Chansons de Bilitis* and the *Ballades de François Villon*, but the modal allusions to an ideal past are now fleeting and teasing, in the same way as Mallarmé's handling of syntax, and in the last song, 'Eventail', gesture and decoration seem as important as any theme, if not more so. If Stravinsky seemed determined to explode his way out of nineteenth-century music, Debussy, shielding himself from the debris, was setting out along a narrow track of his own.

But geniuses rarely go in straight lines for long. So it was that in July Debussy signed a contract to write music for a children's ballet called *La boîte à joujoux* on a story by the artist André Hellé, who specialized in children's books. From grappling with Mallarmé, Debussy now turned to analysing the souls of Chouchou's dolls, whom he found much more sympathetic than humans. The composer Alfredo Casella recalled that 'to the end he remained what the French call *grand enfant* . . . At fifty he amused himself more than did his little daughter Chouchou with the toys brought home for her by her mother.' Like *Khamma*, *La boîte à joujoux* reached the stage only after the composer's death, in an orchestration done mainly by Caplet, so only the payment due on signature found its way into Debussy's increasingly empty pocket.

It is implicit in one or two remarks in his letters that Emma refused to countenance any diminution of the luxurious lifestyle she was accustomed to. At the same time she regularly refused to let him travel without her and no less regularly suffered illnesses of one sort and another: in this summer of 1913 a temperature and accompanying insomnia, which prevented Debussy travelling to London and earning a fairly easy 5,000 francs for accompanying Maggie Teyte in the *Ballades de François Villon*.

It may seem curious to us now that the worldwide success of *Pelléas* did not bring with it any measure of financial security: after all, by the outbreak of the First World War productions of the opera outside France (in chronological order) had been given in Brussels, Frankfurt, New York, Milan, Cologne, Prague, Munich, Berlin, Rome, Boston, London, Chicago, Vienna, Buenos Aires, Geneva, Birmingham and Manchester. Also, in the 1912–13 Paris concert season Debussy's works were played more often than those of anyone except Saint-Saëns.[19] But we need to remember that Durand continued to pay the composer his 6,000 francs a year retainer and that, beyond this, Debussy's debt to Durand rose from 27,000 francs in 1911 to over 56,000 in 1914 (that is, around £2,500 at pre-war prices).[20] Conservatoire camaraderie and genuine admiration for Debussy's genius could take Durand only so far.

There was therefore again no summer holiday for the Debussys. The composer continued to talk to Chouchou's dolls, finishing the piano score of La boîte in October. The Mallarmé songs were published on the 18th and on either side of that date, on 15 and 22 October, Debussy conducted Ibéria. For a production of Gabriel Mourey's play Psyché he had planned several pieces of incidental music, but in the event the premiere on 1 December was graced only by a brief offstage flute solo representing the last notes played by the dying Pan. Published as Syrinx in 1927, 'La flûte de Pan' has become a central piece in the flautists' repertoire and one much analysed by scholars. It may be as well to point out to both parties that Debussy envisaged Pan as a free spirit unacquainted with barlines: these were added on publication by Marcel Moyse.

Debussy did not attend the performance since he left that same day on the longest journey of his married life, the first of five he was to undertake over the next eight months in a final bid for something like solvency. After a gap of thirty years, he returned to Russia. Arriving in Moscow on 3 December, he stayed there for six days, then for three in St Petersburg, then returned for two more in Moscow before leaving Russia on 14 December.

His sponsors were Alexander Ziloti, a cousin and teacher of Rakhmaninov, and Serge Koussevitsky. Although trained respectively as a pianist and a double-bass player, they were on hand both as hosts and as conductors-in-waiting – presumably Debussy's reputation on the rostrum had preceded him. Although there were no musical disasters, Debussy found it hard to sleep and was not helped by letters from Emma. On 6 December, after three bad nights, he wrote back to her:

> What's going to become of us? Your letters are more and more miserable! Like you, I feel nothing will calm you and that makes me very uneasy . . . Once again, I beg you, grant us *both* a little patience and goodwill.

And two days later:

> Do you realize that you wrote: 'I don't know how I'll manage not to be jealous of your music'? Don't you think that's enough to upset one's equilibrium somewhat? . . . The chances are that if I were never to compose again, you would be the one to stop loving me, because I could hardly rely on the somewhat restricted charms of my conversation or on my physical advantages to keep you by me.

Emma's letters to her husband have not survived, so we shall never know whether there were other grounds for complaint which Debussy did not mention. Rumour had it that no pretty girl within 100 metres was safe from him, but Moscow in December was perhaps not the ideal place to exercise such talents. Musically, the trip went well. The *Marche écossaise*, *L'après-midi*, the *Nocturnes*, *La mer* and the clarinet *Rapsodie* pleased audience and critics in both cities and twenty Russian musicians signed an *hommage* assuring him that the happiness they had been counting on from his visit had not eluded them and that 'we have lived with you days that will never fade from our memory'. Did Debussy perhaps think of Berlioz who, likewise ill and exhausted, had forty-five years earlier also found in Russia an unsparing triumph denied him by his compatriots?

During the early months of 1914 the two operas were still under consideration, as were three other stage projects: *Orphée-roi* with Segalen, a one-act ballet *No-ja-li* with Georges de Feure, and an opera-ballet *Fête galante* with Laloy. Debussy actually signed contracts for these last two in November 1913 and January 1914. But he completed none of these and the first six months of 1914 seem to have been totally unproductive.

However he did make three foreign journeys during this period, to Rome, Holland and Brussels. Some idea can be gained of his state of mind from the fact that between leaving Paris for Rome on 18 February and returning there on the 24th he sent Emma twelve letters and telegrams, complaining of her absence, of having no letters from her, of having to leave her to face their creditors, of being in a hotel room in which he felt that 'everything is crumbling round me'. Meanwhile the Roman audience had its doubts about 'Rondes de printemps', but liked *La mer* and especially *L'après-midi*.

After calling in *chez lui* to console Emma and collect some clean shirts, he entrained once more on 26 February for four days in Amsterdam and The Hague, with a fee of 1,500 francs – and again professional success was offset by personal anguish. The day after his arrival in Amsterdam he wrote to Emma:

> The fog is murky (*il fait un brouillard fuligineux*); that's the only
> word for it. I'm again in a dismal state, but with my nerves on edge,
> and I'm off to rehearse.

. . . the word 'fuligineux', or rather 'fuligineuse', comes in the first sentence of Baudelaire's translation of *The House of Usher* and Debussy had already used it as long ago as 6 September 1893 in a letter to Chausson, acknowledging its source.[21] This identification with Roderick Usher, oppressed by fate and the family mansion, may be taken in one of two ways: either Debussy was oppressed by the rigours of travelling and by separation from the one he loved; or else he was oppressed by life, marriage, debts, unfinished (? unfinishable) stage works – by everything, in short, except Chouchou.

He was back in Paris on 2 March, in time to send Pierné some hints towards his second concert performance of *Jeux* four days later: 'I . . . felt the various episodes lacked homogeneity! The link between them may be subtle but it exists, surely? . . . And the last thing, by and large it's too loud' – problems that have continued to dog performances of the work over the last eighty years. Then at the end of April he made his last journey to Brussels, this time as pianist accompanying Ninon Vallin in the *Chansons de Bilitis*.

Shortly after his return to Paris, he was laid up for a fortnight with shingles – often a sign of stress. Then, while the world tried to guess what might follow from the assassination of the Archduke Franz Ferdinand at Sarajevo on 28 June, he made his last journey abroad, to London, to conduct a programme of his works at the Queen's Hall on 17 July: 'Caruso would ask what I'm getting for his accompanist!' he complained to Durand; 'but at least it's a drop of water in the desert of these terrible summer months'.

Debussy's last offering to the old world that war was to shatter for good was a group of six pieces for piano duet, based on the music he had written for Pierre Louÿs's staging of some of the *Chansons de Bilitis* in 1901: he took extracts from seven of the original twelve movements, expanding their 150 bars into 270. The nostalgic beauty of these pieces tempts us to think that Debussy saw the horrors ahead, that this was a last drop of water from the pure well of peace. Maybe. More pro- saically, though, from the fact that he began work on these *Epigraphes antiques* immediately after signing the contract on 15 July and that only half the music had to be newly composed, we may guess that, as always, he needed the money that came not only on signature but on delivery as well. The pieces were indeed finished within a fortnight. Jacques Charlot, Durand's assistant, was expected to collect the last three of them on Friday, 31 July. The next day, France mobilized for war.

7 War and last years (1914–1918)

On 3 August Germany declared war on France. On the 17th a British Expeditionary Force landed on the French coast and on the 26th the French premier, René Viviani, formed a coalition government of national unity: morale in France was high. But German troops had already taken Liège and Brussels and on 5 September, having crossed the French border, they captured Rheims and 12,000 prisoners. By this time the French government had already moved to Bordeaux, and Debussy and his family to Angers to escape the possibility of German bombing. One extract from Debussy's letters may do duty for many on the subject of the Germans and what they symbolized for him. From Angers he wrote to his one-time piano pupil Nicolas Coronio:

> I think we're going to pay dearly for the right to dislike the music of Richard Strauss and Schoenberg . . . When it comes to Wagner, they're bound to exaggerate! . . . Our mistake was to keep trying for too long to follow in his footsteps . . . our generation won't ever be able to change its tastes any more than its forms! What could be interesting and surprising is what those who have fought in this war – who have been 'on the march' in all senses – will do and think? French art needs to take revenge quite as seriously as the French army does!

It soon became clear to Debussy that this flight from Paris had been both expensive and pointless and the family returned home after a fortnight or so. He toyed with the idea of helping the war effort by writing a 'Heroic March', but in fact composed a 'Heroic Berceuse' for piano in November for *King Albert's Book*, 'a tribute of admiration to Belgium' organized in England by Hall Caine and sponsored by the *Daily Telegraph*. He had his doubts about using the Belgian national anthem because, as he wrote to Godet on New Year's Day 1915, it 'stirs no heroic thoughts in the breasts of those who weren't brought up with it', but the result mirrors closely his disillusionment with all wars after his experiences of 1870 and 1871.

This little piece aside, he wrote nothing for the first nine months of the war – a sufficient indication of the numbing effect it had on him. Instead, at Durand's suggestion, he undertook an edition of Chopin's piano works, the German editions now being out of the market because of the war. As he was not a professional in this field, he understandably encountered numerous difficulties, which he tried to alleviate by being rude about his predecessors. Then, on 23 March, his mother died after an illness of a few weeks. While this did not have the drastic effect on him that Ravel felt when his mother died two years later, the fact that Debussy's letters contain no explicit agonizing does not mean that he took it lightly.

In April and May the war took another turn for the worse with the Ypres offensive, the Germans' first use of chlorine gas and, on 7 May, the sinking of the *Lusitania*. In June Debussy helped Emma in her charitable efforts to clothe the wounded by organizing a concert and by writing another short piano piece. But he also began to compose again for himself. On 5 June he started a set of three pieces for two pianos which not only embodies some of his feelings about the war but stands as one of his most extraordinary compositions. On 30 June he wrote to Durand with the hope that the edition of Bach's violin and keyboard sonatas he was being asked to undertake was not urgent – he had 'a few ideas' he would like to follow up. By 7 July the *Caprices en blanc et noir*, as he originally called them, were ready for an 'approximate' performance, had Durand been available to hear it.[1]

But five days later the Debussys left for a three-month stay at a villa, 'Mon Coin', in Pourville. Given the composer's outspoken disenchantment with most previous holiday trips – his general view, as we have seen, was that they were expensive, disruptive and unnecessary – his stay at Mon Coin was little short of miraculous; and, although the terms of it have never been made clear, it is at least possible that the use of the villa was a gift, since Debussy's letters contain no complaints over the expense.

Whether or not such a happy financial arrangement oiled the wheels of his 'thinking machine', these three months were probably the most productive period of his entire life, in terms of both quantity and quality. On 22 July he posted the second of the three movements of *En blanc et noir*, as it now was, to Durand, sealing completion of it in less than seven weeks. He apologized, tongue-in-cheek, for bringing the sixteenth-century chorale *Ein' feste Burg* into conflict with the late eighteenth-century *Marseillaise*, but made no apologies for leaving the outcome undecided: the only winner was War itself.[2]

As a postcript to the accompanying letter, he sent Durand a prospectus: 'Six *Sonatas* for various instruments, written by Claude Debussy, French composer; the first: cello and piano'. In the event, illness and death prevented Debussy from going beyond the third of these six, and of the three he did write the Cello Sonata was the only one that retained its original instrumentation. If this leads us to suppose that a Cello Sonata had been in his mind for some time, we may possibly be right, to judge by the speed with which he composed it: in a letter of 5 August, only a fortnight after he had completed almost the final version of *En blanc et noir*, he could tell Durand that the Sonata would perhaps already have reached him.

Whereas in *En blanc et noir* Debussy had made explicit references to the war, both in the music itself and in the epigraphs at the head of each piece, in the last sonatas he was clearly returning to music written for its own sake – in the above letter he wrote of the Cello Sonata that 'it's not for me to judge its excellence but I like its proportions and its almost classical form, in the good sense of the word'. At the same time he uses timbre as a structural agent in a way which looks forward to later twentieth-century developments, and specifically in his apportioning of *pizzicato*: after a first movement in which the cello plays *arco* throughout, in the second movement (to be mathematical for a moment) some 42 per cent of its bars include *pizzicato*; the last movement (22 per cent) represents a rapprochement between them. Overall, his vision of the cello as a giant guitar moved it decisively and definitively away from its nineteenth-century *legato* inheritance.

Simultaneously with the Cello Sonata he had begun a set of twelve piano *Etudes*, inspired by his editing of Chopin's, which were to occupy him until the end of September. They were his last major contribution to the piano repertoire. They also contain some of his most difficult writing – it is significant that five of the twelve (nos. 2, 5, 6, 9 and 12) were not recorded until after 1950, even Horowitz risking only the relatively easy 'Pour les arpèges composés'.[3] Not surprisingly, there are a number of Chopinesque moments, but in general the language matches the technical demands in its complexity and novelty. And yet through them all runs that playful spirit which was never dormant for long in Debussy's music and which was, no doubt, continually revived by games and conversations with Chouchou. As he told Durand on 12 August: 'these *Etudes* conceal a rigorous technique beneath flowers of harmony (sic). To put it another way, "you don't catch flies with vinegar"! (resic).'[4]

What he called his 'activité de moteur' continued through August and September. Its final efflorescence came in the second of the sonatas of the 'musicien français', for flute, viola and harp. For a brief moment he considered scoring it for flute, oboe and harp, but was soon seduced by the possibilities of having three instruments that are, respectively, blown, bowed and plucked. He himself summed up the astonishing production of these three months in a letter to the Italian conductor Bernardo Molinari, written on 6 October, a week before the Debussys returned to Paris:

> When I tell you that I spent nearly a year unable to write music . . . after that I've almost had to *re-learn* it. It was like a rediscovery and it's seemed to me more beautiful than ever!

> Is it because I was deprived of it for so long? I don't know. What beauties there are in music 'by itself', with no axe to grind or new inventions to amaze the so-called 'dilettanti'... The emotional satisfaction one gets from it can't be equalled, can it, in any of the other arts? This power of 'the right chord in the right place' that strikes you... We're still in the age of 'harmonic progressions' and people who are happy just with beauty of sound are hard to find.

No doubt on his return to Paris Debussy was looking forward to at least a brief rest after this spate of creative activity. It was not to be. On 4 January 1916 he explained to Robert Godet why he had not written for so long:

> I'd been ill for some time: not enough exercise, with the usual consequences, but I could live with those without coming to a halt. Suddenly it all got worse, so they operated; nasty moments and painful after-effects, etc....

From this it looks as though Debussy had been suffering (or thought he had been suffering) for some time from haemorrhoids – presumably from his first painful bout in the early months of 1909. Whether this was the whole story, we cannot now tell. But when the doctors operated on 7 December, it was clear to them that the cancer they found had gone too far to be cured. For the remaining two and a quarter years of his life Debussy used a colostomy.

That same December, En *blanc et noir* was published and a copy found its way into the hands of Saint-Saëns. In the quarter of a century since he had complained of Debussy writing music for orchestra in six sharps, his attitude to his younger colleague had not changed and on 27 December he wrote to Fauré:

> I suggest you look at the pieces for 2 pianos called Noir *et Blanc* which M. Debussy has just published. It's *unbelievable*, and we must at all costs bar the door of the Institut against a man capable of such atrocities; they're fit to stand beside Cubist paintings.[5]

It is entirely understandable that from the viewpoint of someone born in the lifetime of Cherubini, as Saint-Saëns was, En *blanc et noir*

18 Debussy and Louis Laloy preparing to fly a kite

should have signalled the end of civilization, and references to the war cannot, in his eyes, have constituted any excuse. Debussy was never made a member of the Institut.

Among Debussy's visitors in the early months of 1916 were Dukas, Satie and Laloy. It was with the latter that Debussy planned his last project, an *Ode à la France* for solo soprano (Joan of Arc), chorus and orchestra. In 1932 Laloy recalled:

> He had had the idea for a cantata which would describe her [Joan's] compassion, her courage, her sadness, and in the flames of the fire her prophetic faith announcing the liberty of her country after further hardships. He asked me to write the text, and from that time on this was the main, though not exclusive, topic of our all too infrequent meetings. . . . It was during one of these working sessions that he said to me, talking about a strident trumpet call which he had thought of and then abandoned: 'I distrust the exceptional.'

It was in effect by the struggle between that distrust and his desire to reach ever higher that his whole creative life was shaped.

Debussy's existence from here on was, as he surely knew, provisional, with morphine keeping the pain at bay and providing some detachment at least from the world and its problems. Satie came to chat and play backgammon, but money worries continued and his health simply did not permit him to make a suggested American tour. His letters speak of deep depression and on 8 June he wrote plainly to Durand, 'as Claude Debussy can no longer write music, he no longer has a reason for existing'. Then, on 15 July, he received a court order to make a down-payment of 30,000 francs to fund Lilly's alimony of 400 francs a month . . . which he had stopped paying six years earlier! His complaint to his lawyer that, of course, 'an artist is much less interesting than a mannequin'[6] does him little credit, even if it shows how low his spirits had sunk.

On 11 September the Debussys left Paris to stay for six weeks in a hotel at Le Moulleau near Arcachon (where did the money come from?). To Durand the composer sent his usual complaints about hotel life but also, on 17 October, the good news that on a walk along the coast he had 'found the "cellular" idea for the finale of the Violin Sonata' – the third of the six projected sonatas, originally envisaged for violin, cor anglais and piano.

Back in Paris, he went to Durand's house on 10 December to hear a private performance of the Sonata for flute, viola and harp ('by a Debussy I no longer know'), spent some of his sleepless nights reading Chesterton's The Napoleon of Notting Hill, but to Godet pronounced himself 'terrified of planning any sort of work whatsoever – that in itself is enough to condemn it to the waste-paper basket, the cemetery of bad dreams'.

He made a quiet start to 1917, his last full year of life. A chill on his kidneys in February added to his physical problems, while he continued to wrestle with the 'terrible finale' of the Violin Sonata; in which he was helped a little by the fact that the war had reduced the number of the trains which he could hear through his study window. On 24 March he accompanied Joseph Salmon in the first performance of the Cello Sonata, no doubt obeying his own instructions to the pianist that he should indeed accompany and 'not fight against the cellist', and in April finally began on his edition of the Bach Violin Sonatas, suggested to him by Durand the previous summer. On 15 April he penned to Durand his only recorded criticisms of his great predecessor: 'sometimes – often indeed – his prodigious technical skill . . . is not enough to fill the terrible void created by his insistence on developing a mediocre idea whatever the cost!' It is easy to detect in this Debussy's own chronic terror of mediocrity and of the ease with which emptiness can be disguised, at least from some listeners, by a sovereign technique.

This was not a problem that Erik Satie ever had to worry about. In a sense, the essence of Satie's music is that the strength and individuality of his voice come through almost despite the technical naivety, and envy on Debussy's part of the 'naked flesh of emotion' displayed by Satie's music may possibly have lain behind his negative reactions to *Parade*, premiered at the Châtelet Theatre on 18 May. Whether or not Debussy attended the premiere is in dispute, but it looks as though he may have voiced his disapproval earlier because in a letter of 8 March Satie complained to Emma of Debussy's 'painful teasing – and again and again! Quite unbearable, anyhow.'[7] From here on there were no more visits from Satie, for backgammon or any other reason.

At the end of June Debussy was at last able to hear a performance of *La mer* that he liked, by Bernardo Molinari and the Conservatoire Orchestra, and a few days later he and Emma and Chouchou left for his final holiday, at the Chalet Habas in Saint-Jean-de Luz.

He had already made his last public appearance in Paris on 5 May, accompanying Gaston Poulet in the first performance of the Violin Sonata, and in Saint-Jean-de-Luz and Biarritz Poulet again joined him for two more performances – Debussy's farewell to the concert platform. Nor were there to be any more summer miracles on the composing front. On his return to Paris in mid-October, he continued working with Laloy on an operatic version of *Le martyre*, orchestrating *La boîte* and at least thinking about *The House of Usher* and *As you like it*. But, beyond sketches for *Usher*, nothing was achieved. Of the last three sonatas (for oboe, horn and harpsichord; for trumpet, clarinet, bassoon and piano; and for an ensemble of the instruments used in the previous five 'together with the gracious assistance of a double-bass') not even a single sketch survives. His last letter to Durand, dated 1 November, puts the situation succinctly: 'for so many fine projects, I have only this poor health which reacts to the slightest shock, I could say to the slightest change in the weather!'[8]

For the New Year of 1918 he wrote his final letter to Emma, according to her the first time he had put pen to paper for two months. It ended with an enigmatic message worthy of the composer:

> But if it is agreed that love is . . . How will it not be . . .

By now he was bedridden. Cigarettes provided one of his few last consolations, but shortly before his death he was cheered to learn that the Opéra was putting on Rameau's *Castor et Pollux*. The dress rehearsal, Laloy recalled,

> took place on 21 March 1918, in the afternoon, because they were afraid of air-raid warnings in the evenings. It was one of his last regrets not to be able to go to it. Seeing I was leaving, he tried to smile and whispered: 'Say *bonjour* to Monsieur Castor!' Two days later the long-range bombardment of Paris began. During his last days he listened to the dismal sound of explosions, and his suffering ended on Monday, 25 March.[9]

ENVOI

It is a cliché among French composers to claim they have no ulterior motive for composing – not social usefulness, not a desire to be famous, let alone (Heaven forfend!) an eye on the money – and that they write music simply 'as an apple tree produces apples'. Far be it from us to pour scorn on such idealism. But this claim is less an explanation than a warning shot across the bows of any too closely inquiring critic, and as such belongs to the same family as Debussy's more explicit description to Durand of the visit he had from Diaghilev and Nijinsky in August 1912, when he refused to play them what he'd written of *Jeux*, 'not wanting Barbarians sticking their noses into my experiments in personal chemistry!'

Obviously anyone seeking a watertight answer to the question 'Why did Debussy compose?' is doomed to disappointment. But it seems to me that, as long as we are satisfied with answers of the most provisional and approximate kind, the question is still worth asking. No, he did not compose for money, as this account of his life has convincingly demonstrated. With his technique and knowledge of the French operatic repertoire he could, surely, have knocked off a stunning operetta within weeks, but this would hardly have squared with his motto 'toujours plus haut'. No, he had no desire to be famous. The fame *Pelléas* brought him was not welcome and seems to have been one of the factors that drove him into an increasingly hermetic existence in the last fifteen years of his life.

19   One of the last photographs of Debussy

But did he want to be socially useful, perhaps? This is a harder one to answer. It might be truer to say that he wanted to be useful to music, which he likened more than once to an attractive young girl beset by suitors, not all of whom had the purest of intentions. Without question, he regarded much of the music being written in his lifetime as useless: it may have been financially profitable, it may have set feet tapping, but the vast bulk of it fell way below what music could, and in his view should be. In 1905, just a month before the first performance of La mer, he told Louis Laloy that he was laying to rest his critical persona, M. Croche, who, 'rightly disheartened by the musical mores of the age, has passed away peacefully amid general indifference. No flowers or wreaths by request, and above all no music.'

The moral dimension in Debussy's character is impossible to miss. Such a statement might well have provoked laughter in some of his contemporaries who saw only his heartless treatment of at least one mistress and one wife, and were not in a position to understand that these infidelities were caused by his greater fidelity to music: his first wife, by making scenes and slamming doors, disturbed the muse and had to go. But a moral dimension there was and, as often happens, this did not make Debussy particularly kind or tolerant, either in his judgements of others or in what he demanded of himself. And it has been perhaps the chief curse of the label 'Impressionist' that it has led people to concentrate on the delightful surfaces of his music and to miss its rough, dangerous, even cruel undercurrents.

From this duality, indeed plurality, of levels come both the richness and the mystery of Debussy's music. On many fronts, he was a deeply divided composer. For one thing, as we have seen, there was the dichotomy between privacy and publicity. From the ideal sound of a work as heard within his own brain there followed its painful egress into a world of impresarios, performers and gushing admirers – or as he put it to Henri Lerolle in a letter of August 1895, comparing his thoughts about Pelléas with descriptions of foreign countries, 'you build a whole edifice of dreams on them and then reality wipes them out with a merciless sponge'.

This pull between privacy and publicity is mirrored in his struggles to balance the claims of solitude and friendship, and of simplicity and complication. Like the poet Horace, Debussy hated the profane crowd, together with 'universal suffrage and nationalistic phrases', and clung to the company of a few like-minded friends. But whose mind was really like his? With a few exceptions, intimacy had a habit of either shading off into tolerance or turning abruptly to disdain. His longest-serving friend, Robert Godet, was tactful enough to live in Switzerland so that letters could allow Debussy to say just as much as he wanted to say and just as often.

As for the struggle between simplicity and complication, this was possibly the fiercest of all because it related directly to the notes he was trying to put on paper. His love of what he called 'the divine arabesque' can be heard all through his music, from the openings of the symphonic poem *Printemps* and *Prélude à l'après-midi d'un faune* to 'The little shepherd' in *Children's Corner* and *Syrinx*, but he worked relentlessly at finding ways to develop these brief, innocent snatches into music that would not sound relentlessly worked. On his return from a visit to Budapest at the end of 1910, he recommended to his Hungarian friend Barczy that their young composers should learn from gypsy music, 'but don't dress it up in school uniform or put gold spectacles on its nose!'

On a still deeper level, Debussy's music is imbued with a feeling of transience. The dichotomy here is sometimes as much visual as anything. We come into the hall to see a large symphony orchestra, hired at huge expense and wearing respectable clothes. And then they embark on *Jeux* ... So much solid, material presence to produce sounds that are ethereal, evanescent, questioning. Elsewhere the transience of life and love is embedded in the music even more profoundly in that it does not need the magical resources of a large orchestra. What extraordinary sadness the twenty-three-year-old composer was already able to evoke at the end of the song 'Chevaux de bois', as evening falls on the fairground, the whirling wooden horses are stilled and the angelus sounds in the distance! And twenty years later, in 'Colloque sentimental', the same pit of nothingness yawns, bereft of decorative allusions. We know from internal evidence of the impact *Tristan and Isolde* had on Debussy's musical language; no less telling is the message of the opera that love in life and daylight is as nothing compared with love in death beneath the stars.

This reluctance to engage with what the material world calls 'reality' was something that all the women in Debussy's life had to try and accept, with greater or lesser success. One of the things which undoubtedly attracted women to him was his playfulness: examples of it abound in his music, for instance in the wonderful opening bars of his étude 'Pour les cinq doigts' in which a nihilist, mainly blacknote phrase at first seems determined to obliterate a bourgeois, whitenote one. But playfulness too can be seen as a form of transience since the point of games is that they have an end. His profound love for Chouchou surely derived, in part, from the fact that she not only embodied playfulness but could be expected to carry on the playful spirit after his death – Emma no doubt had a lot to put up with and we should perhaps beware of being too hard on her, but playfulness was not one of her attributes. We must see it as one of the mercies of Debussy's increasingly unhappy last years that Chouchou's untimely death, of diphtheria on 16 July 1919, occurred after his own.

As for Debussy's nature pieces, his feeling for transience informs every bar. It is tempting to think that his rude remarks about the Paris Opera building in a newspaper article of May 1901 (railway station on the outside, Turkish bath on the inside) were prompted not merely by Garnier's architecture *per se* but by the fact that it stayed the same summer and winter, season after season. In Nature, on the other hand, everything is in a state of flux. If we were feeling unkind, we could point out that it might be easier for a composer to describe in music the movements of Nature than the non-movement of an opera house. As it is, the sheer class of Debussy's nature painting reduces such a remark to absurdity. It is fair, though, to emphasize that many of his exercises in this domain do deal, not just with the movements of Nature, but with movements down or away from stability or with movements that are circular or cyclic: 'Reflets dans l'eau' may end on a chord of D♭ but our experience of the piece suggests it would need only one small pebble to start the ripples all over again. The flurries of sound in 'Feuilles mortes' are likewise playfully disruptive in feeling, perhaps alluding to the Rackham picture in J. M. Barrie's *Peter Pan in Kensington Gardens* entitled 'There is almost nothing that has such a keen sense of fun as a fallen leaf.'[1]

Finally, from our twentieth-century vantage point, we can see how Debussy anticipated Marshall McLuhan in his perception of the world as a global village. Geographically, his sources ranged from Scotland ('The Girl with the Flaxen Hair') to Spain, and from 'What the West Wind Saw' to the pagodas of China. But in every case, the foreign stimulus is absorbed into the structure, not just pasted on to the outside as some kind of quick exotic fix. Temporally, too, he was a traveller. Rameau was for him little short of a god and Lassus and Palestrina, as already noted in Chapter 2, 'true masters' whose 'melodic lines unroll and expand, reminding you of the illuminations in ancient missals' – this at a time when all three composers were largely ignored by the French musical world at large. But through it all, it is Debussy's moral dimension that strikes home again and again. Love, beauty, the present are all transient, the past and future foreign countries. Bereft of religious faith, Debussy nonetheless kept faith with music. As with Bunyan's pilgrim, no foes could stay his might, though he fought at every step with the giants of ridicule, indifference and incomprehension, and, as one of a small handful of composers, made good his right to be a pilgrim, marching towards the music of the future.

As for Debussy's relationship with his successors, this deserves a book to itself. For the moment I cannot do better than quote Pierre Boulez:

> Varèse and Webern were the first to learn the lesson of Debussy's last works and to 'think forms', not – in Debussy's words – as 'sonata boxes' but as arising from a process that is primarily spatial and rhythmic, linking 'a succession of alternative, contrasting or correlated states' – that is to say, intrinsic to its object but at the same time in complete control of it.

... while of *Pelléas et Mélisande* Boulez makes a claim which might, with barely an exception, be applied to Debussy's mature œuvre as a whole:

that it belongs in the very highest class, the class of works that serve as a kind of mirror in which a whole culture can see itself transfigured.[2]

Boulez wrote those words over a quarter of a century ago; but the mirror remains, for those with eyes to see.

1 Childhood and musical studies (1862–1884)

1 Letters of 9 December 1851 and 16 January 1852, *Correspondance générale d'Hector Berlioz*, IV, ed. Pierre Citron (Paris, 1983), pp. 92, 102; *Selected Letters of Berlioz*, ed. Hugh Macdonald (London, 1995), pp. 282, 283.

2 Letter of 9 January 1856, *Correspondance*, p. 240; *Selected Letters* p. 338.

3 *Selected Letters* p. 406.

4 *La passion de Claude Debussy* (Neuchâtel, 1962); tr. William Ashbrook and Margaret G. Cobb as *A Portrait of Claude Debussy* (Oxford, 1990).

5 'Memories of Debussy and his Circle', *Recorded Sound* 50–1 (1973), p. 161.

6 Louis Laloy, *Claude Debussy* (Paris, 1909), p. 11.

7 Letter of 1 September 1915, *Lettres de Claude Debussy à son éditeur* (Paris, 1927), p. 150.

8 Albert Lavignac, *L'éducation musicale* (Paris, 1902; 7/1918), pp. 1–2.

9 For details of Debussy's Conservatoire assignments and a more sympathetic view of *Le gladiateur*, see John R. Clevenger, 'Achille at the Conservatoire 1872–1884', *Cahiers Debussy* 19 (1995), pp. 3–35.

10 François Lesure, 'Debussy et la Concordia (1883–1885)', *Cahiers Debussy* OS 3 (1976), p. 5.

2 Roman holiday? (1885–1887)

1 *Debussy: His Life and Mind*, 2 vols. (London, 1962, 1965), I, pp. 66–7.

2 'Debussy lecteur de Banville', *Revue de musicologie* 46 (1960), p. 211.

3 Henri Rebois, *Les grands Prix de Rome de musique*, (Paris, 1932), p. 60.
4 The diary is in the Musée Hébert, Paris. The following extracts are taken from François Lesure, *Claude Debussy* (Paris, 1994), pp. 78, 87, 88.
5 Lesure, *Claude Debussy*, p. 85.
6 Igor Stravinsky and Robert Craft: *Memories and Commentaries* (London and New York, 1960), p. 30.
7 Humphrey Carpenter, *Benjamin Britten* (London, 1992), p. 278.
8 'Formulaic Openings in Debussy', *19th Century Music* 8 (Summer 1984), pp. 44–59.
9 *Debussy* (Paris, 1956), p. 96.
10 *Les arts français* 16 (1918), p. 92.
11 *Impressionism* (London, 1967; 2/1973), p. 234, and plate of *Les grandes baigneuses*.

3 A Bohemian in Paris (1887–1893)

1 'Debussy à dix-huit ans', *La revue musicale* 7 (1 May 1926), pp. 21–2.
2 Letter of 17 March 1887, in François Lesure, *Claude Debussy* (Paris, 1994), pp. 88–9.
3 Letter to the directors of 7 September 1887, in Frédérique Patureau, *Le palais Garnier dans la société parisienne 1875–1914* (Liège, 1991), p. 243. Much of the detail in the following paragraphs comes from this excellent book.
4 'Exposition de la Royal Academy', *Gazette des Beaux-Arts* 2 (1869), pp. 44–61; cited in Richard Langham Smith, 'La genèse de *La damoiselle élue*', *Cahiers Debussy* 4–5 (1980–81), pp. 4–5 and two following quotations.
5 quoted in François Lesure, *Catalogue de l'œuvre de Claude Debussy* (Geneva, 1977), p. 63.
6 *Debussy and Wagner* (London, 1979), p. 42. See pp. 22–42 for a full and fascinating discussion of the Wagnerian influence on *La damoiselle*.
7 *Claude Debussy*, p. 94.
8 'Richard Wagner et Tannhäuser', *Revue européenne* 1 (April 1861).
9 The poem *La musique*, no. LXIX of *Spleen et idéal*.
10 *Debussy and Wagner*, pp. 42–3.
11 in full in a, fairly free, English translation in Edward Lockspeiser, *Debussy: His Life and Mind*, 2 vols. (London, 1962, 1965), I, Appendix B, pp. 204–8.

12 Teresa Davidian, 'Debussy's *Fantaisie*: Issues, Proofs and Revisions', *Cahiers Debussy* 17–18 (1993–4), p. 22.

13 The work has been edited by Richard Langham Smith and a CD recording issued on Erato Musifrance 4509-98508-2.

14 *Les compagnons de la Hiérophanie* (Paris, 1937), p. 73. As Robert Orledge notes in *Satie the Composer* (Cambridge, 1990), p. 340, n. 9, the frequent references to Villiers de l'Isle Adam in the previous section 'mean that Satie and Debussy must have met before 1889, for this was the year the poet died'.

15 'Réponse à Jules Huret', *Œuvres complètes* (Paris, 1951), p. 871; quoted in Andrew Thomson, *Vincent D'Indy and his World* (Oxford, 1996), p. 75.

16 *Le chant des voyelles comme invocation aux dieux planétaires* (Paris, 1912; Nice, 1976), p. 23; quoted in English translation in Joscelyn Godwin, *Music and the Occult* (Rochester, NY, 1995), pp. 153–4.

17 Demar Irvine, *Massenet: A Chronicle of his Life and Times* (Portland, OR, 1994), p. 161.

18 'Debussy's Settings of Verlaine's "En sourdine"', *Perspectives on Music*, ed. Dave Oliphant and Thomas Sigal (Austin, 1985), pp. 231–2.

19 Thomson, *Vincent d'Indy and his World*, pp. 80–1.

20 Pierre Bernac, *The Interpretation of French Song* (London, 1970), p. 194.

21 A full list of the twenty-four questions with Debussy's handwritten answers is in Jean Barraqué, *Debussy* (Paris, 1962), p. 72.

22 Léon Vallas, *Claude Debussy et son temps* (Paris, 1958), p. 151.

4 Scandals and masterpieces (1894–1901)

1 Diary entry, February 1894; quoted in François Lesure, 'Debussy à travers le journal de Madame de Saint-Marceaux (1894–1911)', *Cahiers Debussy* OS 3 (1976), p. 5; letter of 5 February.

2 François Lesure, 'Claude Debussy, Ernest Chausson et Henri Lerolle', *Humanisme actif. Mélanges d'art et de littérature offerts à Julien Cain* (Paris, 1968), pp. 341–3.

3 *Debussy: His Life and Mind*, 2 vols. (London, 1962), I, p. 166, n. 1.

4 Henri Borgeaud, ed., *Correspondance de Claude Debussy et Pierre Louÿs (1893–1904)* (Paris, 1945), pp. 122–3, n. 2.

5 For full details see Robert Orledge, *Debussy and the Theatre* (Cambridge, 1982), pp. 305–29.

6 *La passion de Claude Debussy* (Neuchâtel, 1962), pp. 118–19; Eng. tr. William Ashbrook and Margaret G. Cobb as *A Portrait of Claude Debussy* (Oxford, 1990), pp. 96–7.

7 Robert Cardinne-Petit, *Pierre Louÿs intime, le solitaire du Hameau* (Paris, 1942), p. 145; quoted in Arthur B. Wenk, *Claude Debussy and the Poets* (Berkeley, 1976), p. 176.

8 Hélène Jourdan-Morhange, *Ravel et nous* (Geneva, 1945), p. 166.

9 See Roger Nichols, *Debussy Remembered* (London, 1992; 2/1998), p. 108, n. 4. The question of Debussy's interest in the Dreyfus Affair is fully discussed in Déirdre Donnellon's unpublished M.Phil. thesis, 'Debussy in the Political and Social Context of his Time' (University of Liverpool, 1995), Chapter 2 and especially pp. 56–61.

10 Nicolas Nabokov, *Old Friends and New Music* (London, 1951), p. 150.

11 François Lesure, *Claude Debussy* (Paris, 1994), p. 189.

12 See Jean-Pierre Barricelli and Leo Weinstein, *Ernest Chausson* (Westport, CT, 1955), p. 105 for a list of thirty names.

13 *La passion de Claude Debussy*, p. 135.

14 See Nichols, *Debussy Remembered*, p. 150, n. 4.

15 Letter to Florent Schmitt of 8 April 1901. Arbie Orenstein, *Maurice Ravel, Lettres, Ecrits, Entretiens* (Paris, 1989), p. 64. An arrangement of the whole work for two pianos was published under Ravel's name in 1909.

16 *Les écrits de Paul Dukas sur la musique* (Paris, 1948), pp. 529–33.

5 Idol and victim (1902–1907)

1 Letter to the editor of *Le figaro*, 14 April 1902.

2 Mary Garden and Louis Biancolli, *Mary Garden's Story* (London, 1952), pp. 63–4, 68.

3 Maurice Emmanuel, *Pelléas et Mélisande* (Paris, 1925), p. 64.

4 quoted in Marcel Dietschy, *La passion de Claude Debussy* (Neuchâtel, 1962), p. 153.

5 *The New York Times*, 16 May 1909; article reprinted in David Grayson, 'Claude Debussy addresses the English-speaking World', *Cahiers Debussy* 16 (1992), pp. 24–5.

6 quoted in François Lesure, *Claude Debussy* (Paris, 1994), p. 255.

7 Bibliothèque Nationale Rés. Vmf. ms. 53.

8 *The Musical Times*, 1 September 1904, p. 600.

9 Aloys Mooser, 'Heurs et malheurs du *Prélude à l'après-midi d'un faune* à Saint-Pétersbourg', *Cahiers Debussy* 16 (1992), p. 65.

10 Robert Craft, 'Prince Igor's Dance', *The Times Literary Supplement*, 13 September 1996, p. 3.

11 *Debussy in Proportion: A Musical Analysis* (Cambridge, 1983), pp. 70–135.

12 Roy Howat, foreword to *Œuvres complètes de Claude Debussy*, vol. III (Paris, 1991), p. XVIII.

6 Travels and travails (1908–1914)

1 *Expositions and Developments* (London, 1962), p. 138.

2 *Claude Debussy* (Paris, 1994), pp. 313–14.

3 C.-F. Caillard and J. de Bérys, *Le cas Debussy* (Paris, 1909), pp. 9, 12–13, 40.

4 Paul Landormy, *La musique française de Franck à Debussy* (Paris, 1943), pp. 230–1.

5 See Roger Nichols, *Debussy Remembered* (London, 1992; 2/1998), p. 328, n. 2.

6 Letter to Jean Marnold of 7 May 1910. Arbie Orenstein, *A Ravel Reader* (New York, 1990), p. 117.

7 Edward Lockspeiser, *Debussy: His Life and Mind*, 2 vols. (London, 1962, 1965), II, p. 129 n. 4.

8 Michael de Cossart, *Ida Rubinstein* (Liverpool, 1987), pp. 29–30.

9 *Debussy and the Theatre* (Cambridge, 1982), p. 217.

10 'Debussy Discusses Music and his Work', *New York Times*, 26 June 1910; David Grayson, 'Claude Debussy Addresses the English-speaking World', *Cahiers Debussy* 16 (1992), p. 25.

11 Richard Buckle, *Nijinsky* (London, 1980), p. 282.

12 'Claude Debussy à Rome'; François Lesure, 'Une interview romaine de Debussy', *Cahiers Debussy* 11 (1987), p. 5.

13 *Stravinsky* (London, 2/1979), p. 209.

14 Jacques Durand, *Quelques souvenirs d'un éditeur de musique*, 2 vols. (Paris, 1925), II, p. 126.

15 'A propos des "Images" de Claude Debussy', *Les cahiers d'aujourd'hui* 3 (February 1913), pp. 135–8; pp. 366–8, n. 6.

16 E. Stoullig in *Le monde artiste*. L. Vallas, *Claude Debussy et son temps* (Paris, 1958), pp. 393–4.
17 Information from the late Mary Antonietti, who met Debussy in London in 1909.
18 *Debussy on Music*, collected and introduced by François Lesure, tr. and ed. Richard Langham Smith (London, 1977), p. 295. For Debussy's contacts with Inayat Khan, see R. Howat, 'Debussy et les musiques de l'Inde', *Cahiers Debussy* 12–13 (1988–9), pp. 141–52.
19 E. Hurard, 'Aperçu sur le goût musical à Paris en 1913', *L'année 1913*, I (Paris, 1971), p. 521.
20 Lesure, *Claude Debussy*, p. 355.
21 *Revue musicale*, 1 December 1925, p. 117.

7 War and last years (1914–1918)

1 *Lettres de Claude Debussy à son éditeur* (Paris, 1927), pp. 134–5.
2 see Jurjen Vis, 'Debussy and the War: Debussy, Luther and Janequin', *Cahiers Debussy* 15 (1991), pp. 31–50.
3 Margaret G. Cobb, *Discographie de l'œuvre de Claude Debussy* (Geneva, 1975), p. 50.
4 See Roger Nichols, *Debussy Remembered* (London, 1992; 2/1998), p. 145, n. 1.
5 C. Saint-Saëns and G. Fauré, *Correspondance*, ed. J.-M. Nectoux (Paris, 1994), p. 115.
6 F. Lesure, *Claude Debussy* (Paris, 1994), p. 397.
7 R. Orledge, *Satie the Composer* (Cambridge, 1990), pp. 65–6.
8 See Nichols, *Debussy Remembered*, p. 190, n. 1.
9 *La musique retrouvée* (Paris, 1928), p. 228.

Envoi

1 (London, 1906), opposite p. 12.
2 *Orientations*, ed. J.-J. Nattiez (London, 1986), pp. 371 and 317.

Debussy's own writings

Debussy on Music, collected and introduced by François Lesure, translated and edited by Richard Langham Smith (London, Secker and Warburg, 1977). A collection of Debussy's newspaper articles and interviews.

The Poetic Debussy, edited by Margaret G. Cobb (Rochester, NY, University of Rochester, 1982; 2 rev/1994). The complete texts of Debussy's songs with critical annotations, and a selection of relevant letters.

Debussy Letters, selected and edited by François Lesure and Roger Nichols, translated by Roger Nichols (London, Faber and Faber, 1987).

Monographs and articles

Léon Vallas: Claude Debussy, His Life and Works, translated by Maire and Grace O'Brien (Oxford University Press 1933; 2/1973). Originally published as Claude Debussy et son temps (Paris, Alcan, 1932; 2 rev/1958). The first detailed study in English.

Edward Lockspeiser: Debussy (London, Dent, 1936; 5/1980). A life and works study in the Master Musicians series.

Arthur B. Wenk: Claude Debussy and the Poets (Berkeley, University of California Press, 1976). A thorough examination of the composer's treatment of his song texts.

Robin Holloway: Debussy and Wagner (London, Eulenburg, 1979). A composer's view of the links between two other composers, with many convincing music examples.

Roger Nichols: 'Debussy', *The New Grove Dictionary of Music and Musicians* (London, Macmillan, 1980).

Robert Orledge: *Debussy and the Theatre* (Cambridge University Press, 1982). The definitive study of this topic.

Roy Howat: *Debussy in Proportion: A Musical Analysis* (Cambridge University Press, 1983). A provocative thesis claiming, with a wealth of documentation, that Debussy based some of his works on mathematically derived structures.

Arthur B. Wenk: *Claude Debussy and Twentieth-century Music* (Boston, G. K. Hall, 1983). A useful study of Debussy's music in the context of what came after it.

David A. Grayson: *The Genesis of Debussy's Pelléas et Mélisande* (Ann Arbor, UMI Research Press, 1986). The definitive study of this topic.

Roger Nichols and Richard Langham Smith: *Pelléas et Mélisande* (Cambridge University Press, 1989). A volume in the series Cambridge Opera Handbooks.

James R. Briscoe: *Claude Debussy: A Guide to Research* (New York and London, Garland, 1990). An invaluable reference book, including information about individual works and an annotated bibliography.

Oscar Thompson: *Debussy, Man and Artist* (New York, Dodd, Mead, 1940). Not always reliable as to fact, but often stimulating.

E. Robert Schmitz: *The Piano Works of Claude Debussy* (New York, Duell, Sloan and Pearce, 1950; 2/1966). Schmitz was himself a fine pianist who studied with the composer.

Edward Lockspeiser: *Debussy: His Life and Mind*, 2 vols. (London, Cassell, 1962, 1965; 2/1978). Still one of the liveliest and most thought-provoking of Debussy studies.

Frank Dawes: *Debussy Piano Music* (London, BBC, 1969).

David Cox: *Debussy Orchestral Music* (London, BBC, 1974).

Stefan Jarocinski: *Debussy, Impressionism and Symbolism*, translated by Rollo Myers (London, Eulenburg, 1976). Originally published as *Debussy, a imprezionizm i synmbolizm* (Warsaw, Polskie Wydawnictwo Muzyczne, 1966). Deals ably and thoroughly with this thorny question.

Marguerite Long: *At the Piano with Debussy*, translated by Olive Senior-Ellis (London, Dent, 1972). Originally published as *Au piano avec*

Claude Debussy (Paris, Julliard,1960). Contains some interesting insights, even if the author rather overstates the importance of her place in the composer's life.

Mme G. de Tinan: 'Memories of Debussy and his Circle', *Recorded Sound* 50–1 (1973). The author, the Dolly of Fauré's *Dolly Suite*, was Debussy's step-daughter.

Marcel Dietschy: *A Portrait of Claude Debussy*, edited and translated by William Ashbrook and Margaret G. Cobb (Oxford, Clarendon Press, 1990). Originally published as *La passion de Claude Debussy* (Neuchâtel, Editions de la Baconnière, 1962). With Lockspeiser's volumes, the most incisive and thoughtful treatment of the composer's life and attitudes.

Roger Nichols: *Debussy Remembered* (London, Faber and Faber, 1992; 2/1998). A collection of reminiscences by Debussy's friends and contemporaries.

Simon Trezise: *Debussy: La mer* (Cambridge University Press, 1994). A clearly written and wide-ranging study of this masterpiece.

Richard Langham Smith, ed.: *Debussy Studies* (Cambridge, University Press, 1997). A collection based on papers given at an international Debussy conference in London in 1993.